CHRISTINA PESOLI

BREAK FREE FROM THE DIVORTEX

Power Through Your Divorce and Launch Your New Life

SEAL PRESS

BREAK FREE FROM THE DIVORTEX
Power Through Your Divorce and Launch Your New Life
Copyright © 2014 Christina Pesoli

SEAL PRESS
A Member of the Perseus Books Group
1700 Fourth Street
Berkeley, California 94710

Library of Congress Cataloging-in-Publication Data

Pesoli, Christina
Break free from the divortex : power through your divorce and launch your new life / Christina Pesoli.
pages cm

ISBN 978-1-58005-535-2 (paperback)
1. Divorce--Psychological aspects. 2. Self-actualization (Psychology) I. Title.
HQ814.P467 2014
155.9'3--dc23
2014009240

10 9 8 7 6 5 4 3 2 1

Cover design by Faceout Studio, Kara Davison
Interior design by Tabitha Lahr

Printed in the United States of America
Distributed by Publishers Group West

To Margaret and Aaron Terwey, and to Angela and David Peterman, whose relationships reaffirm my faith in marriage (no pressure!)

To Hannah Brannon, who takes my breath away (in a good way, mostly)

To Clint Harbour, who has no idea how great he is (which totally works in my favor)

To Peter Pesoli Sr., who teaches by example (even still)

Contents

Introduction

● ● ●

Getting to Know You

(And by You, I Mean Me)

Congratulations!

That's probably not what you were expecting the opening sentence of this book to be, given that it's about divorce recovery. But, trust me, congratulations are in order. Sure, you're facing a divorce and that's about as much fun as running a marathon with two blown knees. Not that I've ever run a marathon. Or blown a knee. But I *have* lived through more than my fair share of divorces. Anyway, that's not why I'm congratulating you. I'm congratulating you because, divorce nightmare notwithstanding, you are loved.

How do I know? Someone cared enough about you to get you this book. Either that, or you got it for yourself, which tells me you are taking good care of yourself and that's equally awesome.

However you came to possess *Break Free from the Divortex*, you now hold the key to reclaiming your power and unlocking your future. So keep this book handy because you're going to need it to get from where you are now to where you're going next, which is going to be *way* better. I promise.

I also know you are lovable. It's easy to forget this when you are at the onset of a divorce. After all, when the very person you thought would love you forever is now hiring a lawyer against you, it's hard not to take it as a referendum on your lovability. And that rejection can send you into a tailspin of self-reproach. You go around and around, blaming yourself for everything you did or did not do when you were married, and how all those things may have contributed to where you are now. But this is not the time to get bogged down in blame. (We'll sift through your mistakes later and mine them for any lessons they hold before we permanently lay them to rest.) What happened happened. You are where you are. Mistakes don't mean you are not lovable; they mean you are human.

You are also lucky—much luckier than I was at the start of my last divorce. (The fact that I've had more than one shows how well qualified I am to write this book, not how poorly qualified I am to maintain a romantic relationship.) But before I tell you about what a disaster my last divorce was, I have to fill you in on the one before that—the one where everything went smoothly.

About fifteen years ago, I finally changed my answer from "I do" to "I just can't anymore." My husband and I had been married for thirteen years, but the last couple of those years included a separation or two and a trial reunion. We had shared some fantastic years together and managed, without even trying, to produce the most amazing son ever born. But we had married young and as the years passed we ended up in two very different places, with conflicting visions of what we wanted the rest of our lives to look like.

I wanted to be on an upwardly mobile track, complete with a bigger house and a car with a functioning air conditioner. He wanted to downsize so he could dedicate more time to training for marathons. I believed in things like establishing retirement accounts and setting up a college fund for our son, Aaron—rules that I thought were a mandatory part of responsible adulthood. He rejected many of these rules and also bristled at conventions such as having health insurance and wearing shoes in the grocery store. But our biggest issue was this: I wanted to have another child and he was happy with just one.

After years of butting heads over an ever-growing list of disagreements, I came to realize that these weren't matters of right or wrong; they were matters of personal belief and individual choice. Rather than forcing one person to bow to another's worldview—and the life plan that went with it—I came to the conclusion that the kinder and healthier choice was to let each other go.

For the record, the foregoing account is my take on what happened in our relationship. I'm pretty sure he has a different view and it goes something like this: After he stuck with me through college and law school, I dumped him. Rather than debating our conflicting accounts of why we divorced, I instead consider this further confirmation of how differently we saw the world.

If we were divided on how to be married, we were surprisingly united on how to get divorced. Neither one of us was out to hurt the other, no one was in a hurry to move on to another relationship, and, most important, we were both determined to shepherd Aaron through the process while protecting his relationship with each of his parents.

We both regularly attended Aaron's sporting events and school activities, and occasionally the three of us even went to dinner together afterward. We hardly tangled over the custody schedule and let Aaron split time between our two houses based largely on what worked best for everyone. I'm not saying it was a cakewalk. But as far as divorces go, it was as close to nontoxic as you can get and no one benefited from that more than Aaron.

I came away from that experience vigorously patting myself on the back. I was awesome! I knew how to get divorced while protecting my son from all that was negative about the process. Why couldn't everyone handle divorce as brilliantly as I had?

Eventually I remarried, and my then-husband (whom I'll refer to herein as either "my ex" or "That Man") and I had a beautiful baby girl. Hannah was a gift from heaven, but the marriage was straight out of hell. With each passing year, it descended to a lower, darker level, until I finally realized that if we didn't get a divorce, I would not be in the requisite mental and emotional state to take care of myself, let alone parent my daughter.

The marriage was grueling, but the divorce was even worse. My ex did plenty of jerky things while we were together, but once we separated he cranked up the jerkiness to 11. It was brutal from start to finish. And I learned tons of things as a result.

I learned, for example, that I was a credit hog. Much of the praise that I had lavished on myself for how well my last divorce had gone belonged to Aaron's dad, not me. I realized that it only took one person to make a divorce toxic, but it took two people to keep things positive. And if you're not the one who wants the divorce but you still manage to be decent about the whole thing, you deserve a far bigger share of the credit.

I learned that I was strong. Not "I can lift a car with only my index finger" strong, but Girl Power strong. The years I spent in a bad marriage had definitely caused me to forget that. It took me a while to remember I had once possessed that strength and even longer to summon it again. But once I did, I could handle just about anything.

I also learned that I was human. Despite my best efforts, I still made mistakes. I was okay with that as long as I studied them for whatever lessons they held and did my best to avoid repeating them.

Finally, I learned that I was powerful. Who I was and what I did from that moment on were up to me. I wasn't going to hand any of my power over to my ex by letting him push my buttons. I wasn't going to waste any of my present obsessing over the past. There was an open road ahead of me, and I was ready to punch the accelerator and move forward.

Then I started to get phone calls and emails from other women. Perhaps because I am a lawyer, or because my divorce was so nasty, or because I'm not stingy with my opinions, for whatever reason I started hearing from friends—and friends of friends, acquaintances, and even the occasional stranger.

These women weren't looking for legal advice—after all, I didn't practice family law. They were looking for directions. They wanted to know how to break free from what I call the "divortex" and get on with their lives. What's the divortex? Good question. (Don't bother to look it up on Wikipedia. It's not there yet, but I'm working on that.) The divortex is the gravitational pull that forces all your thoughts and energy to endlessly orbit around your divorce and your ex. (We'll circle back to this concept later. Pun intended.)

As I listened to their stories, I noticed some very clear patterns—common mistakes women made that not only cost time and money but also jeopardized custody issues and settlement outcomes. In the process they were seriously imperiling their futures.

I realized that there is a dangerous chasm between the domain of divorce lawyers and the theater of therapists. In this unmapped territory, no one is there to lead the way because divorce lawyers are too expensive and therapists are not always mindful of the ramifications of certain behavior when you're a party to a lawsuit. (And no one should ever forget that a divorce *is* a lawsuit.) In this no-man's-land, women often stumble into traps and trip over land mines that complicate their divorces and drive up their legal bills, and this in turn causes them to get really mad at their lawyers.

To help women find their way forward, I wrote a series of articles called "Divorce Boot Camp." The response I got led me to develop a curriculum to help women get through their divorces and back on their feet. And Emotional Hardbody Divorce Boot Camp was born.

Emotional Hardbody Divorce Boot Camp seeks to do for divorcing women what childbirth class does for women who are pregnant: provide an overview of what they're up against and help them to prepare for what life will be like in the future. The classes also offer social support by connecting women with others who are in the same boat.

I began hearing from women who wanted to attend Divorce Boot Camp but either didn't live in the area or couldn't afford the tuition. They always asked the same question: Was there a book I could recommend? Finally, the answer to that question is yes. *Break Free from the Divortex* is a survival manual for women who feel cut off at the knees by their divorce, which brings me to one more thing I know about you: Your divorce is hitting you hard. Maybe it's because you didn't see it coming. Maybe it's because the problems had been slowly building up for years. Maybe it's because he was controlling, or a cheater, or emotionally unavailable, or a narcissist—or all of the above. Why your divorce has knocked you flat doesn't matter. The fact that it has makes this the book for you.

So, here we are. You need help and I am here to provide it. Let's get started.

PART ONE:

HOUSTON, WE HAVE A PROBLEM

1.

Ground Zero

(Welcome to the Worst Time of Your Life.
Don't Unpack Your Things.)

Divorce sucks. In fact, it sucks so much you can't even enjoy the life-threatening amount of weight that you'll drop in the process. Most of us are happy whenever we see any downward movement on the scale. But when the weight-loss formula is massive amounts of stress and soul-crushing despair, no one really feels much like celebrating. It's sort of the opposite of happy hour: You're anything but happy and the experience lasts a lot longer than an hour.

People refer to this phenomenon as the "divorce diet." But that term doesn't begin to do the whole experience justice. The weight loss comes with a not-so-complimentary makeover that includes bags under your eyes and a haggard "scarecrow chic" look—all scary and nothing to crow about.

During my divorce, people would often comment on all the weight I was dropping. Notice I said "comment," not "compliment." The truth was, I didn't take the remarks as compliments. I had mirrors in my house. I could see what I looked like. And I sure knew what I felt like. These remarks only added insult to injury—as out of line as commenting on the accidental loss of a limb. No one would ever say, "Wow, your arm is completely gone! That chainsaw just cut it clean off!"

That's how it felt to me during the initial days of my divorce, as if I was trying to go through the motions of everyday life (shopping, returning library books, picking up my daughter from school, making dinner) with one arm shorn off and blood gushing everywhere. I knew my gaping wound was obvious, but I sure didn't want the librarian to comment on it.

All of this is to say that I understand where you are right now, because I have been in the exact same place and remember what it was like in painful detail. I'm not going to insult you by sugarcoating it: You're at Ground Zero. Your life has been blown to bits and you are knocked flat. You feel dazed, stunned, and beat up. You don't even know if it's worth the effort to try to crawl out from under the burning wreckage that was your marriage because you don't know where to go from here. Your normal life is gone and you don't have anything to replace it.

Here's some good news: I also know where I am now. I am thousands of miles away from my Ground Zero, right smack in the middle of my new normal life—a life that I really love. It is a gazillion times better than my Ground Zero, but it is also infinitely better than what my life was like before I got a divorce.

The best part is that I paid careful attention along the way, taking notes and sketching a detailed road map, so I know exactly how I got from Ground Zero to my new normal life. I'm not going to just hand all that information over to you; I'm going to do something even better. I'll be your coach to get you into shape for the expedition and then I'll be your cocaptain on your trek from Ground Zero to your new normal life. I will be equal parts friend, drill sergeant, personal trainer, BFF, and tour guide. Sometimes you'll love me; other times you might hate me. But you will always be able to trust me to lead you in the right direction—away from dysfunction and despair and toward health and happiness.

You don't have to simply take my word for this. After all, going through a divorce can make you wonder whether you can trust anyone, let alone someone you've just met. So, I'm going to give you a tool you can use to chart your own progress and verify that you're heading in the right direction. It's called the Calendar Trick.

Have you ever been in an exercise class in which the instructor has everyone doing repetitions of something really hard—like pushups—but she doesn't give you any clue when she's going to stop torturing you? When you have no idea how many pushups you're expected to do, you're likely to quit after ten. But if she tells you up front that you're doing three sets of fifteen, you are more likely to be able to hang in there for all of them.

I've found that's true whenever you're doing anything difficult. If you don't know how long the misery is going to last, it's tempting to just throw in the towel. But if you know how long you're expected to take the pain, then you can pace yourself and make it through.

This is where the Calendar Trick comes in handy. Today's date is your personal Ground Zero. Grab a calendar and mark the date with whatever symbol you feel is fitting—a frownie face, a bomb, or a steaming pile of dog poo. Then, flip ahead and circle the date exactly six months from today and decorate that day with something more upbeat, such as a cupcake or a star, for example. Finally, flip ahead another six months (a full year from your personal Ground Zero) and mark that date with something even better, like a bottle of champagne, balloons, or confetti—dealer's choice.

As time goes by, note milestones or positive progress on your calendar: the date you unpacked your last box in your new house, the deadline when you turned in all the documents your lawyer requested in order to answer a discovery request, the first weekend without your kids you didn't cry. This calendar is for noting "up" days and forward progress, not "down" days or backsliding.

There is no way of knowing right now exactly how long your divorce is going to take from start to finish. (If you follow all my advice, you will be doing your part to ensure that it goes as quickly as possible. And if your ex also behaves, there's an excellent chance you can wrap it up in six to twelve months.) Even though you don't know exactly when your divorce will be over, the sheer passage of time has tremendous healing power. When you get to the six-month mark, you will feel worlds better than you do today, even if your divorce is not final. When you get to the one-year anniversary, you will be blown away at how far you've come and how much better your life is already—and the trajectory goes up from there.

In the meantime, whenever you are having a low day, get out your calendar. Count the days or weeks that have passed since your personal Ground Zero. Think about how you felt during those first few days, consider how far you have already come, and appreciate how much you have already accomplished. Look at how much closer you are to those six- and twelve-month milestones. Having a calendar that reflects completed milestones you can take pride in and future milestones you can look forward to will help you realize that, however terrible things might seem at the moment, the bad times will not last forever. Time is your ally because each and every day it moves you further away from your personal Ground Zero and toward the launch date of your new life.

Ground Zero Flashback

Before we move forward, I want to tell you about my Ground Zero. Before I moved out of the house I "shared" with That Man, there were things I knew and things I didn't know. I knew that my marriage was badly broken. I knew that That Man was truth-challenged and had control issues. I knew he was jealous of my son from a previous marriage. When That Man told me that Aaron—a self-supporting recent college graduate—could only stop by the house to visit two times a month, I knew I had to leave.

What I didn't realize at the time was just how harrowing the whole divorce would be. It's not as if I expected it to be a walk in the park. After all, I was very aware of the personality I was dealing with. But I guess I thought the relief and happiness would always outweigh the stress and despair. That was not the case.

That's why I was so surprised when shortly after I moved out, two uninvited houseguests muscled their way into my new home. Their names were Fear and Sadness. Before then, I wasn't really on a first-name basis with either of them, but, once the divorce was under way, they were my constant companions for a few very long months.

Sadness showed up first. She arrived the very weekend I was moving out. That Man and I had agreed that our daughter, Hannah, six years old at the time, would stay with him while I got things unpacked and set up her room. I thought the point was to minimize the stress and disruption for her. But That Man thought it was an excellent opportunity to introduce Hannah to his new lady friend—the one with whom, his cell phone records later made clear, he was already quite well acquainted.

Sadness saw my empty house and decided to make herself at home. She had a way of making me cry. A lot. It wasn't that I was never happy during this time. Despite my uncertain future, I was tremendously relieved that I no longer had to live in the same house with That Man. Even though I was worried about what I was putting my daughter through, I understood intellectually that divorce was the only answer and I was proud that I had mustered the courage to begin the process.

That didn't stop Sadness from bullying me. She would follow me around from room to room. I would jump in my car to get away from her, but she always managed to come along for the ride. When I was having lunch with a friend or pushing my grocery cart through the produce aisle, she would pop up out of nowhere and make me start crying again. And the fact that I was crying over a divorce I knew was really the only option for my kids and me made me even more depressed.

I felt like the cartoon character in that TV ad for Zoloft— the one who has an individual-size rain cloud hovering over her head indoors and out, threatening a downpour at any time. But unlike the person in the TV commercial, I never got to the part at the end where the sun comes out and the cloud disappears. My personal weather forecast for those few months was always "despondent with a chance of sobbing."

Shortly after Sadness moved in, Fear showed up. Sadness pretended not to know him, but I wasn't fooled. They worked like a team. Fear had me worrying about everything. How was I going to support myself? Where would I get health insurance? How much of an emotional toll was the divorce taking on Hannah? Could my ex really get custody of her, as he was threatening? During the day, my exhaustion made it that much easier for Sadness to push my buttons. And come nightfall, being emotionally wrung out made it easy for Fear to rattle my cage all night long.

My ex saw my weakened state and tried his best to exploit it. He closed my bank account without my knowledge and changed the beneficiaries of life insurance policies in contravention of court orders. He altered our tax return so that our tax refund—which amounted to tens of thousands of dollars— would be directly deposited into his separate bank account. He wined and dined his new lady friend, buying her cowboy boots and an iPod and taking her on trips, all financed with community funds. I felt as if I was in a game of divorce Whac-A-Mole, not knowing what the next jerk move would be or which direction it would come from.

After a few months, I realized that Fear and Sadness were hijacking my time with Hannah. I was so preoccupied with them that I was unable to really focus on my daughter when she was with me. I was broody, moody, mopey, and terrified, and I could see it was wearing on her.

Then something crystallized for me. I hadn't managed to send Fear and Sadness packing because I couldn't muster the strength to do it for myself. But my inability to get the upper hand was causing Hannah to feel further unsettled at a time when her life was already in turmoil. Once I recognized this, I knew that regardless of whether I was able to banish these emotions for me, I had no choice but to do it for her.

As I tried to figure out a war plan, two additional guests—Anger and Humor—showed up at my door. At first I was unnerved by these additional intruders. I already had an emotionally full house; I didn't have room for more pity-party crashers. But it didn't take long for me to figure out that Anger and Humor had enlisted as soldiers in my war against Sadness and Fear. And I knew I could use all the help I could get.

Anger took on Sadness and it was really no contest. Sadness's display of tears not only failed to evoke any sympathy from Anger but actually served to enrage her. Every time Sadness tried to pull one of her little stunts, Anger was ready with a swift kick.

Whenever Fear tried to spook me, Humor was right there making fun of him. In the middle of the night, Fear would shake me awake and tell me that I wasn't going to be able to support myself. But Humor always pushed back. "Oh, right! With only a law degree she probably won't be able to get a job anywhere. Such a shame." Fear would slink away emasculated, his thunder totally stolen from him.

The first couple of weeks of this were fantastic. Anger and Humor were my own personal superheroes. Watching them win round after round with Fear and Sadness, which had been sapping all my strength for months, was thrilling. The dynamic duo generated power—power that helped me stand up for myself and my daughter, and fight back.

Anger and Humor kicked Sadness and Fear out of the house and locked the door. Then they trained me so that I knew what to do should those two ever dare to show up again. Suddenly, I felt much better. I was sleeping fine. I was laughing again. I was fighting my own battles. I was back.

The vibe in the house improved seemingly overnight, and Hannah perked up immediately. The sun finally broke through the clouds of that antidepressant commercial that I had been trapped in for months. Hannah could count on me to be a source of strength again—a role model for Girl Power. I was standing on solid emotional ground and, more important, so was she.

The Importance of Being Angry

I knew it wouldn't be healthy for Hannah to see me go through something as major as a divorce from her father and look as if I didn't even miss a beat. But the problem is, sadness has a very short shelf life when it comes to its usefulness. If it lingers too long, it can be really counterproductive. You stay mired in the past. You feel lousy about yourself and your future. You can't make decisions. It saps your strength and drains your motivation for embarking on new projects. In short, it prevents you from getting over your divorce and moving on.

But anger is a different story.

My former hairstylist first pointed out how these two emotions differ in usefulness. She told me about a friend whose husband had failed to make their house payments for several months and spent all their savings without her knowing it. Then, just as the house of cards was collapsing around them, he up and left her and the kids. A couple of months later when I was in for another haircut, I asked how her friend was doing.

"Not well," she replied. "She's still sad. She needs to get over being sad and move onto being mad. Then she can start getting things done."

I was fascinated by this analysis. Once I stopped to think about it, I was surprised at how many women followed that pattern. They experienced crippling sadness at the onset of their divorce, but then later graduated to anger and a burst of productivity, personal growth, and healing immediately followed. Singer-songwriter and 2012 Grammy Award hoarder Adele is a great example. She went through a bad breakup and at first she was crushed. But then she got mad. She harnessed that power and used it to create an album that swept up every award for which it was nominated. Although famous people's success stories can be inspirational, they can also seem removed from our everyday lives. It's often more empowering to hear stories of triumph from ordinary people because they are easier to relate to, and Kelly's story of post-divorce triumph fueled by anger is my favorite.

Kelly always had an interest in acting, but, with three kids and a husband whose job required him to travel a lot, she never had the time to pursue it. Plus, acting was something for which her husband had low regard. After all, being an actor in local theater productions was not an endeavor that would make any real money—the only measure of value he recognized. To him, acting seemed like both an ego trip and a pipe dream all mixed together. If she wanted to do something that would make some money, such as selling real estate, he would have been all over that. But acting? Not only was he not supportive of the idea, he couldn't hide his disdain for it.

Not surprisingly, Kelly and her husband eventually split up. It turns out that, while he was away on business and she was at home with the kids, he had developed some outside interests of his own. These interests had names like Crystal and Kandi and were creative enough to compose steamy texts, but not smart enough to keep straight which nights he was out of town and which nights he was at home with Kelly and the kids.

The divorce hit Kelly hard. She spent the first few months adrift and forlorn. The kids were older, so she had sizable chunks of time on her hands. Then she got mad. She was mad that she had shelved her own interests in order to appease her husband. She was mad that, while she was at home clipping coupons, helping the kids with homework, and making sure everyone got three square meals a day, he was in cities like Las Vegas and Los Angeles wining and dining the likes of Crystal and Kandi with family funds. But it was the fact that she had spent months moping around after splitting up with such a jerk that made her really furious—at herself.

She recognized that she needed to do something with all that anger. To move on, she needed a project to throw herself into, so she signed up for an acting class and converted all that anger into energy for her new craft. This was a critically important step.

She wasn't trying to become famous so she could show her ex. She was pursuing something that she enjoyed for herself. She wanted to get past being mad over her divorce and mad at herself for putting her own interests last for so long. She figured that a good way to do this was to pick an interest and prioritize it.

Not surprisingly, things really took off. Her acting teacher connected her with an agent and before she knew it, she was getting cast in local TV commercials. She found a new set of friends, she loved what she was doing, and the money she was making from her new hobby was a nice supplement to her regular income. She was so busy that she didn't even notice exactly when she stopped being angry. And being sad was such a distant memory it seemed like a whole lifetime ago. Kelly was finally happy. That's when she knew she had turned an important corner in her divorce.

The story could have stopped there and it would have been a happy ending all by itself. But this is one of those delicious tales that ends with both extra icing and a huge cherry on top. Kelly was cast in an ad for a local hospital and a huge photo of her smiling face was plastered on a billboard alongside a busy highway—on the exact stretch that her ex-husband and many of his coworkers drove every morning to get to work. As they say in the movie business, "Roll the credits. That's a wrap."

And speaking of raps, it seems like anger always gets a bad one. Popular psychology tells people that in order to heal, they have to let go of their anger. But that advice is misleading. The thing is, anger is a lot like gasoline. Gasoline can both burn your house to the ground and make your car go.

The same is true of anger. If it's not handled the right way, it can destroy you. But if you harness its power and make it work for you rather than against you, anger can propel you to do incredible things. If you follow the conventional wisdom and simply let go of your anger, you've just walked away from a very valuable resource. It's like throwing away a gift card for a year's supply of free gasoline.

Be careful not to confuse helpful anger with her trashy and

destructive cousins, rage and obsession. Rage tries to get you to do negative things such as slashing your ex's tires or keying his car. Obsession leads to stalker-type behavior such as fixating on your ex's every move. Neither rage nor obsession has any place in healthy divorce recovery. If you discover either of these losers taking up residence in your head and you can't quickly usher them out by yourself, find a good therapist on the double.

As Adele put it in one of her six Grammy acceptance speeches in 2012, breaking up from a "rubbish relationship" is something everyone experiences. You have to work through your sadness but not get stuck there. Eventually, you will turn the corner from sad to mad and, when you do, make sure to treat your anger like a rocket ship. Pointing it at your own house would be self-destructive. Targeting it at your ex's house would keep you focused on your past. Instead, choose an exciting new destination and aim it in that direction. And remember, when you're traveling by rocket ship, the sky is the limit.

Countdown to Liftoff

I told you not to unpack your things. After all, Ground Zero is no place to settle in. The conditions are incredibly harsh and not at all conducive to sustaining healthy human life. So, we'll be shipping off immediately. This is Day One of your odyssey to your new normal life.

Just as astronauts and athletes have to endure rigorous training, so do you. The chapters that follow will train you up while coaching you through. Some days you'll feel that you've made huge progress, and other days you'll feel as if you're spinning your wheels or maybe even losing some ground. There will be intense challenges along the way, and at times you will wonder if you have it in you to go the distance. I'll be there to remind you that you do. Although we'll do our best to navigate around it, there will be some turbulence. But the overall trajectory for you from this point is up, not down. You do your part and I'll do mine, and your divorce will go faster and cost less, and every day you will get closer to the finish line. Together we will get you to your final destination—and you're going to love it there.

Now turn the page so we can blast off and be on our way.

2.

The Lowdown on Lawyering Up

Once you have made the decision to get a divorce (or the decision has been made for you by your soon-to-be ex), the first item on your "to-do" list is to hire a lawyer. The initial step of calling an attorney to schedule a consultation can be surprisingly daunting. Even though I am a lawyer and have no shortage of lawyer friends, the thought of calling a divorce lawyer to set up an appointment crippled me with fear. I knew it was something I had to do—sooner rather than later—but I still couldn't bring myself to dial the number. Day after day, I kept making excuses to put it off.

I felt like I was confronted with a horse with a broken leg. It was obvious that the horse was in pain. I knew it was not going to get better, and the only humane and responsible thing to do was to put the horse down. But that didn't make pulling the trigger any easier. I just couldn't do it. It seemed so irreversible.

Not to beat a dead horse, but in this tortured metaphor the mortally wounded horse represents a terminally ill marriage and calling a lawyer is tantamount to pulling the trigger. There I was—immobilized and terrified. I worried that I'd be putting events into motion that I wouldn't be able to stop, even though I knew there was no other option.

Chances are you feel the same way. If so, here's what you don't realize: Even though making that call is really hard, once you've done it you will instantly feel relieved. I'm not saying all your stress will melt away, but I promise you will feel at least a little, and quite possibly a lot, better. Because once you've made that call, rather than feeling that (brace yourself for a change in similes here—we're going from equestrian to nautical) you are adrift in the marital equivalent of the Dead Sea, you'll feel as if you've made contact with the Coast Guard and there's a rescue boat headed your way. (This might be a good time to tell you that I am a huge fan of similes and metaphors—and I'm not above mixing them. So, gird your loins and prepare for takeoff.)

Making that first call to set up a consultation with a lawyer takes some pretty big ovaries. (In this book, rather than using the tired and off-the-mark term "balls" as a euphemism for courage, we're going with the much more appropriate term "ovaries." And if that wigs you out, it's time for you to grow a pair.) Once you take that first step, each subsequent step will get progressively easier.

In case you're still feeling paralyzed by the prospect of diving in, I'm going to give you an assignment that will buy you a little time. But first there are two nagging issues we need to get out of the way:

1. Do *not* try this at home. In case you are one of those people wondering whether hiring a lawyer is really necessary, the answer is—as Sally in *When Harry Met Sally* would say—"Yes, yes, yes, *yes*, YES!" Do you know the saying, "The lawyer who represents herself has a fool for a client"? Well, the opposite is also true: The nonlawyer who represents herself has a fool for a lawyer.

Your divorce has the potential to affect virtually every aspect of your life—from how much time you get to spend with your kids, to how much say you have in their lives, to how much time you have alone, to where you live, to what you own, to how much money you have now, to what you owe, to whether and how you can retire. The outcome of your divorce can have a ripple effect that lasts until you draw your last breath.

When you stop to consider the magnitude of this, the thought of just winging it without someone in your corner who actually knows the legal landscape and is not emotionally invested in the outcome of your case is as irresponsible as it is crazy. And no, mooching free advice from a lawyer friend does not count as representation.

A client once told me she didn't need a lawyer because she and her husband didn't own anything and the only money there was to divide up was what her mom left to her when she passed away. She was prepared to fork over half the funds she inherited to her ex and walk away. What she didn't realize was that since her husband's profitable construction company was started by him after they got married, it was community property and half hers. But the money she inherited from her mom was by law separate property and therefore entirely hers. Because she didn't know the rules, she didn't know how to identify what items were and were not part of the community estate.

If you don't know what comprises the community estate, how can you hope to accurately calculate your fair share? You would never hear someone say, "I have cancer, but I'm just going to treat it on my own and avoid the expense of going to a doctor." You only get one shot at this divorce. There's no do-over if you represent yourself and botch the outcome. So, act like the grownup that you are and handle your case responsibly.

2. Fight for your fair share of the community estate. If I had a dime for every time I've heard a woman going through a divorce say, "I don't care about the money. I just want to have my kids as much as possible," I would have plenty of extra money to give away. And I'd give it to each of these women. Lord knows they could use it, because more often than not they have a really hard time making ends meet.

I understand this sentiment. I even expressed it myself over and over again during my divorce. Luckily, my lawyer still fought for my share of the community estate, realizing that the custody split was most likely going to be the standard arrangement anyway.

Other women aren't so lucky. Their future exes bully them with threats about getting custody of the kids and then these otherwise smart women panic. They focus only on the fight for custody and take their eye off the ball when it comes to the details of the community property split. When the dust settles, they end up with standard custody but are financially strapped. In the final analysis, they've hurt both themselves and the kids they wanted so desperately to protect.

In fact, your financial settlement does more than affect your kids' quality of life while they're under your roof. If you can't take care of yourself financially in your old age, it will likely fall to your kids to help you out then, too. So do right by your kids and don't let your ex's scare tactics throw you off. Fight for your fair share when it comes to both the community estate and custody of the kids.

Know How to Pick 'Em

Maybe you didn't do a great job of picking whom to marry. But that doesn't mean you can't do a good job of picking the lawyer to represent you in your divorce. You've heard of the three Rs of education, right? Well, there are also three Rs of hiring a divorce attorney—reflect, reach out, and research. Following these steps will help you choose the right lawyer to represent you.

REFLECT

Before you buy a vehicle, you have to be clear on your transportation objectives. Lots of questions come into play, such as do you normally fly solo or do you have a squadron of kids to shuttle around? Is your ego tied to your ride or can you handle the constant humiliation of being seen behind the wheel of a minivan? Do you work from home or do you face a daily commute from the suburbs to downtown? As these questions indicate, it's not simply a matter of getting from point A to point B. A Hummer and a Fiat 500 can both get you from one place to another, but one is perfect if you're into Berettas and the other is good if you're into baristas.

Before you decide what lawyer to hire, you need to be clear on your divorce objectives. Sure, you want a lawyer who can get you unmarried. But beyond simply changing your marital status, what other outcomes do you expect from this process? Below are some possible answers. After some honest reflection, circle the ones that apply to you:

- Get through the divorce quickly.
- Keep the legal bills low.
- Have your kids with you as much as possible.
- Trash your ex's reputation.
- Turn your kids against your ex.
- Get a good division of community property.
- Make your ex's life a living hell.
- Leave your ex penniless and miserable.
- Get sole custody of the kids, no matter what.
- Take everything that matters to your ex, whether or not you want it.
- Protect your kids from the emotional fallout of your divorce.
- Be in a position to take care of yourself and your kids financially and emotionally.
- Make your ex sorry he ever met you.
- Get your divorce behind you as quickly as reasonably possible so you can begin the next chapter of your life.

Depending on the circumstances and your wiring, you may be hoping for any or all of these things right now. Because you're human and divorce is as traumatic as it is personal, this is understandable. I am not going to lecture you on what outcomes you should or should not fantasize about wanting from your divorce. Realistically, it's way too soon to expect you to have worked through all of your negative feelings. But it's not too soon for you to be able to identify which expectations are healthy and reasonable, and which are not. Here's how that list breaks down:

Healthy and Reasonable

- Get through the divorce quickly.
- Keep the legal bills low.
- Have the kids with you as much as possible.
- Get a good division of the community estate.
- Protect your kids from the emotional fallout of your divorce.
- Be in a position to take care of yourself and your kids financially and emotionally.
- Get your divorce behind you so you can begin the next chapter of your life.

Crazy and Corrosive

- Trash your ex's reputation.
- Turn your kids against your ex.
- Make your ex's life a living hell.
- Leave your ex penniless and miserable.
- Get sole custody of the kids. (This could be in the "Healthy and Reasonable" column if your ex has a history of abuse or neglect.)
- Take everything that matters to your ex, whether or not you want it.
- Make your ex sorry he ever met you.

The trick is to let only the healthy, reasonable desires factor into how you select your divorce lawyer and approach managing your case. Do you want to get divorced with the least amount of drama, trauma, and expense, or are you itching for a huge fight so your marriage can go down in a blaze of whatever the opposite of glory is? Are you looking for a fair division of the community estate, or do you want to take your ex to the cleaners so that he ends up living under a bridge and panhandling for his next meal? Answering these questions will determine what qualities you'll need your lawyer to have.

A skilled but levelheaded attorney would be well suited to de-escalate conflict and engage in firm but constructive negotiations. (And, by the way, being levelheaded is not the same as being a pushover.) A lawyer who acts like a pit bull would be an excellent choice if you want to go for your ex's jugular, clamp down hard, and not let go until he bleeds out, along with all of the money. A lawyer who believes that children need to be protected from the battle, rather than put on the front lines, can help you craft a custody arrangement that both protects your kids' best interests and respects your role as mom. An attorney who thinks winning is everything will view your kids like another possession up for grabs—and getting them is important to his win/loss record, regardless of the toll it takes on everyone else.

After giving all of this some thought, if you still find yourself motivated by a desire for revenge, remember there are plenty of lawyers who will gladly act as assassins rather than advocates. But this will cost you in at least three different ways:

1. Your legal bills will be higher. And the higher the bills, the less money you'll have to fund launching your new life, since both parties' legal bills are typically paid out of community funds.

2. Your divorce will take longer. Having knock-down, drag-out fights over every issue rather than trying to compromise eats up a lot of time and ultimately delays putting your divorce behind you once and for all.

3. You and your ex will end up hating each other forever. The more your lawyer takes a scorched-earth approach, the more you will damage your relationship with your ex, and the less likely you'll be able to get along in the future. You may not care about that now, but, if you have kids together, you will quickly realize how important that is—not for profound reasons but for practical ones. It's less "Namaste" and more "Please switch days." Plus, not hating your ex makes it much easier to co-parent, which in turn dramatically lessens everyone's stress level—including that of your kids.

Even if your ex hires a pit bull lawyer to represent him, it's *still* a bad idea to hire one for yourself. The only thing worse than having one pit bull lawyer in your divorce case is having two. This isn't about taking the high road; it's about minimizing the damage and trying to ensure that your portion of the community estate goes to you rather than your lawyer. Two of these lawyers on the case will result in twice as much money being wasted on ginned-up legal fees, twice as much time being spent on unnecessary fights, and twice as much animosity being engendered between you and your ex. No smart shopper wants anything to do with "two-fer" specials like that. If your ex hires a pit bull, your objective should be to hire a divorce lawyer who is tough but not obstinate—someone who is not the type to throw sucker punches, but not afraid to block blows and swing back when necessary.

When it comes to your divorce, I'm not saying you have to rid yourself of all your anger and negative feelings toward your ex. As we discussed in the previous chapter, those emotions can be useful—but not when you're choosing your divorce lawyer. If you let your anger and negative feelings drive the decision of whom you hire to represent you, don't be surprised when your divorce goes off the rails. So, make smart, conscious choices about how to lawyer up.

REACH OUT

Now that you're clear on your divorce objectives, the next step is to reach out to your friends and acquaintances for referrals. Start by asking friends if they can recommend any divorce lawyers, both in terms of whom to use and whom to stay away from. Don't limit yourself to friends who themselves have gotten a divorce. Your happily married or blissfully single friends may also have great feedback on local divorce lawyers from friends and family who have gone through the process.

When you ask for these recommendations, don't stop with asking whom they do and don't recommend; be sure to follow up by asking why. The "why" part will give you insight into whether the particular lawyer will be a good match for you and your divorce objectives. When gathering these referrals, factor in the personalities of the people providing them. A recommendation from your reasonable friend is qualitatively different from the one you get from your belligerent boss.

Don't be surprised if some people end up recommending their ex's attorney rather than their own, which serves as both a recommendation of the former and an indictment of the latter. Be sure to drill down on this and find out the basis for your friends' opinions on both attorneys. Because when it comes to recommendations, researching who not to use and why can provide equally valuable data.

As you talk to friends who have gotten divorced, think back to how they acted before, during, and afterward. If two friends both seemed like reasonable people when they were married to each other but then morphed into monsters during their divorce, it could be that the personality transformation was due to the temporary insanity that comes with splitting up. It could also be that one or both of them had the kind of lawyer who specializes in whipping things up rather than smoothing things over.

It's true that most people don't have a lot of good things to say about their ex during or immediately after a divorce, but time usually tamps down the hate. If years after the divorce is over, those same reasonable friends despise each other more than ever, that's an indication that they may have had some not-so-professional help in creating that animosity.

While we're talking about the afterglow of negative feelings, keep this in mind, too: It is very common for a person to dislike her lawyer immediately following the conclusion of the divorce. Part of this is topic fatigue. You reach a point where you are sick and tired of your divorce and everything associated with it. In addition, it takes a while to come to terms with the reality that no matter how good a job your lawyer does, not every single thing will go your way.

When the ink on your decree hasn't even dried, it's easy to focus on what you lost and blame your lawyer. Over time, a more balanced assessment usually emerges. So, if you are getting mixed reviews about a lawyer, consider whether the negative ones are coming from someone who just finished her divorce. If so, take that into consideration when weighing her opinion.

RESEARCH

There are four factors that have the most influence over whether your divorce will be smooth sailing—with the occasional stretch of choppy waters—or the legal equivalent of Hurricane Katrina from start to finish. Those factors are you, your lawyer, your ex, and your ex's lawyer. You can control only two of them—you and your lawyer. So, it makes sense to do everything you can to maximize your half of this equation.

The work you've done reflecting and reaching out should leave you in a position to come up with a short list of possible candidates. Armed with this information, it's time to dig deeper into each one.

Experience. Many people think of practicing law as a one-size-fits-all occupation, like being a plumber or working as a cashier. But law is more like medicine in that there are many areas of specialty. Just as you wouldn't go to a podiatrist to get a breast cancer screening, you shouldn't hire a criminal lawyer to handle your divorce.

Not only do you have to hire a lawyer who practices family law, but you also need to consider how much experience she has and whether your case has any special complexities. If you haven't been married long and you don't have any property, debt, or children, you can go with a less experienced lawyer. But if you invented Spanx and your wealth subsequently ballooned as quickly and dramatically as your waistline during your last pregnancy, you're going to need a lawyer with both experience and snap.

When it comes to complexities, type matters. Valuing and dividing oil and gas royalties is a different exercise than valuing and dividing an Internet startup. If there's a divorce lawyer who has built a good reputation handling divorces that involve complicated estates similar to yours, that lawyer should be on your list of attorneys to interview. If you know a couple who owned a few Taco Bells and got divorced after the husband made a run for the border with a hot tamale, and you and your hubby made your dough from a chain of Pizza Huts, be sure to interview each of their lawyers. Whenever you can use the research someone else paid for to supplement your own, so much the better.

Personality. Your divorce will require you to talk about highly personal subjects at a time when you feel more vulnerable than ever. It goes without saying that you need an attorney with whom you feel comfortable. Topics such as your sex life, your worst parenting moments, your biggest meltdowns—and anything else embarrassing that you and your ex assumed (or even promised) you would both keep private—are now potential topics for deposition questions and public filings. The best way to figure out if you would feel comfortable talking about these matters with someone is to schedule a consultation.

Feeling comfortable with your lawyer also requires not feeling as if you're being talked down to by her. You expect your lawyer to know more than you, you want your lawyer to be frank with you, and at times she may even disagree with you. But at no time should she talk down to you. Although you don't expect to be coddled, you don't need to be insulted, either.

When you schedule the consultation, pay attention to how you feel about your interactions with everyone you encounter along the way, including the receptionist, secretary, and legal assistant. It is likely that you will spend more time talking to them than you will with your actual attorney, and that's not necessarily a bad thing when you consider the difference in hourly rates. Oh, and if a lawyer won't even talk to you before putting you through an asset screening with one of her underlings, then she's more interested in your money than your case.

Personalities are multifaceted. Many lawyers have one persona socially, perhaps another when talking to clients, and quite possibly a completely different one when interacting with opposing counsel. Don't be swayed by friendly banter if sources have told you that a certain lawyer's style is aggressive to the point of being obstinate. You do want a lawyer who can be a strong advocate, but you don't want one whom others find impossible to work with because that will cost you time and money.

One last consideration about personality: In addition to how comfortable you feel with your lawyer and how well your lawyer plays with others, so to speak, you may wonder if you should take into consideration how your ex will react to your choice. For example, if your ex is a chauvinist blowhard, you may think that hiring a male attorney is necessary to keep him in check. Or if your ex is reputation-obsessed, you may conclude that hiring a lawyer who occupies a position of prominence in your same social circle will keep your ex from acting like a jackass.

The thing to remember here is that while your ex will read letters and documents drafted by your attorney, he will rarely, if ever, have any direct interaction with your lawyer. As a result, concerns over how your ex will react to factors like these should rank lower on your overall list. There is one area, though, where your ex's reaction to your choice in lawyer can have a big impact. If you hire a lawyer with a reputation of going for the jugular, that decision can scare your ex into hiring a lawyer with a similar reputation. And once that happens, neither of you should be surprised when you emerge from your divorce broke, bloody, and bitter.

Price. Getting divorced is going to set you back some and that's scary enough. But what's even scarier is that you can't know in advance how much. This makes it feel as if you're being asked to sign a blank check and, the truth is, you are. People tend to want to blame the lawyers for this, but that's not fair. There is no way for a lawyer to know at the beginning of your case how long or how complicated your divorce will be. To ask a lawyer to give you a firm price on your divorce before it's done is like asking a homebuilder to quote you a firm price before he knows whether the house is going to be a cozy two-bedroom bungalow or a mansion big enough for Brangelina and their brood of kids.

Your lawyer should be able to give you an educated guesstimate based on factors including:

- whether you own property together, and, if so, how much and what type,
- whether either of you is self-employed,
- whether either of you owns a business,
- whether you have minor kids and, if so, how old they are,
- what types of personalities are involved,
- whom your ex has hired to represent him,
- and whether both parties want the divorce.

But there are a myriad of variables that she cannot control, including how you act and react, how your ex acts and reacts, and whether your ex's divorce lawyer tries to stir the pot.

Because they have no idea what twists and turns your case might take, lawyers bill by the hour. The billable rate can vary dramatically from city to city and even from lawyer to lawyer within the same city. It stands to reason that lawyers with more experience have higher billable rates than those with less experience, but another important factor to consider is overhead. It will come as no surprise that a lawyer who has fancy downtown digs will charge more than an equally experienced attorney who works out of his house. But consider this: The lawyer with an actual office is likely to have a legal assistant and a secretary, whereas the lawyer working from his home office may not. And legal assistants have billable rates that are significantly lower than the lawyers for whom they work, and work performed by legal secretaries may not be charged to clients at all.

The lawyer who works from home may end up doing all the work at his billable rate, even filing and going to the post office, whereas the lawyer with the downtown office will delegate that work to his legal assistant and secretary. However, it may be standard practice for the big firm to charge you for every single photocopy—after all, that view from the high-rise is not going to pay for itself—whereas the solo practitioner may absorb a lot of those costs himself.

I'm not saying that one setup is better than the other. I'm saying there's more to the analysis than meets the eye. Make sure you understand what charges are passed on to you, who will be doing what work, and at what rate. Then decide what's important to you. If having a sweeping view of the downtown skyline while meeting with your lawyer is a priority, you might have to put up with monthly bills that include charges for each and every binder clip—and those binder clips might cost so much you'll wonder if they're made of gold. But if you don't like getting stuck with talking to the legal assistant when you call your lawyer, you might have to put up with meetings at your local Starbucks rather than a swanky conference room.

You now have all the information you need to select the lawyer who is best suited to handle your divorce. If after reading this, you decide to disregard my warnings and hire a lawyer with a reputation for being overly aggressive, I have one more piece of advice for you: Make sure you pick a lawyer who likes to travel. That way, when your divorce is over and you're broke because all your money went to cover your attorney's fees, you can at least look forward to receiving a photo Christmas card from her last exotic vacation and take some comfort in knowing that you helped pay for that.

3.

Lawyers, Bills, and Money
(Getting the Most Out of Your Representation)

There's nothing quite like the feeling you get when you hire a divorce lawyer. Well, actually, there is. It's called love. Sure, writing the check for the retainer hurts. But aside from that, you will come away from this first official meeting feeling as if you've fallen head over heels.

Just as the love you once had for your ex wasn't permanent, the love you now feel for your lawyer will wear off, too—only faster. Don't despair. This is a normal part of the divorce process. The key is to expect this so that when it happens, you don't misinterpret it or overreact.

There are three things that can kill the love between you and your lawyer:

1. At the beginning of the relationship, you attribute powers to your attorney that simply aren't reasonable. Finally, you found someone who *gets* you! Your depressed days and terrified nights are forever over! You now have someone who is going to be really, really *there* for you! Your lawyer completely understands what a tool your ex is and how mistreated you've been! If your ex tries to pull any stunts, she will totally have your back!

Your lawyer's job is to do the legal work to dissolve your marriage. She is not your personal bodyguard, your big sister, your therapist, or your new best friend. However great your lawyer is, she is not a superhero. As time wears on, you will begin to see that your lawyer is human and comprehend the limits of what she can do. And you will be disappointed.

2. The bills from your lawyer will hit you wrong. No matter how reasonable they may be, the bills are always higher than you expect. And even though you clearly understood when you signed that check for the retainer that this was a business relationship, the nature of the material you cover and the fact that she sees you at your most vulnerable tend to make it feel more personal than business. When you get the bill, you are reminded of the truth: This is ultimately just business to her. You feel just a little bit betrayed and you think less of her. You know you shouldn't, but you still do.

3. Second only to your ex, your divorce lawyer will become the face of your divorce (and you will reach the point where you absolutely hate looking at that face). At first, you couldn't wait to see her and you would have talked to her all day, if you could have afforded it. But eventually you will despise any interaction you have to have with her. This is actually a good thing because it is a sign that you are ready to move on with your life.

Reaching this point is common; the danger is that you won't recognize it as a normal part of the process, and you may mistakenly conclude that you may need to fire her. Switching lawyers midway through your divorce costs time and money. Sometimes it's necessary—and when you have to, you have to. But before you fire your lawyer, make sure that what you're experiencing isn't the normal souring that goes along with working through the stages of your divorce.

Managing Your Relationship

The expression "Time is money" may not have been inspired by lawyers, but it certainly applies to them. When it comes to your representation, you should definitely get what you pay for. But the opposite is also true: You have to pay for what you get.

Know when the meter is running. Lawyers bill for their time. Whenever a lawyer spends time working on your case, you will have to pay for that time. Phone calls, text messages, and emails count as much as researching issues and drafting documents. If you fire off a dozen text messages to your lawyer each day, you can't cry foul when charges for reading and responding to them show up on your bill.

In addition to knowing what your lawyer's hourly rate is, you need to know her minimum billing increment, too. Some lawyers bill in quarter-hour increments, whereas others charge in tenths. It might not seem like that big a difference, but depending on how you manage (or mismanage) your communication, it can have a huge impact on your bill.

Let's say you send your lawyer an email asking her a question about your kids' spring break schedule and she responds with a two-sentence email answering your question. Further assume that the whole thing took her five minutes—one minute to read your email, one minute to check your temporary orders, and three minutes to fire off a response. If her billable rate is $350 an hour and her minimum billable increment is fifteen minutes, that answer will cost you $87.50 and you paid for ten minutes of time that you didn't use. In other words, you just wasted almost $60. But if her minimum billable increment is six minutes, that answer cost you $35 and you only squandered one minute of time (or about $6). It's not hard to see how this can add up.

Understanding how this works and managing your communication accordingly can result in significantly lower legal bills, more efficient communication, and a better overall experience.

Don't have your lawyer on speed dial. Rather than picking up the phone or firing off an email to your lawyer every time a question pops into your head, adopt a policy of sending a weekly roundup instead. Have a running list of less urgent matters you want to discuss. Then pick a day of the week—say Friday, for example—to email the list to your lawyer and stick to that schedule. If something major or urgent happens (your ex cancels all your credit cards), by all means let your lawyer know immediately. But if it's not a pressing matter (such as a question about whether you'll need his written consent to take the kids to your cousin's wedding in Europe next summer), put it on the list for the weekly roundup. Then, each Friday before emailing the list to her, review everything you've written down. If some matters have resolved themselves in one way or another, delete them from the list.

Who you gonna call? It is very important for you to be able to tell the difference between developments that you need to pass along to your lawyer and the garden-variety divorce garbage that may affect you and your mood but doesn't impact your case. Your ability to learn this distinction will have a direct impact on how low the drama and the legal bills stay, and how smoothly and quickly your lawyer can get your divorce done. You don't want to fail to tell your lawyer something significant, but you also don't want to get billed for filling her in on something you really only needed to tell your best friend.

To help you get the hang of this, we're going to play a game. I want you to read each of the following scenarios and decide whether you think the situation merits a call to your lawyer, your therapist, or your BFF (or all three). If you think it merits telling your lawyer, the next question is whether it's something your lawyer needs to know as soon as possible or if it's something that goes on your weekly roundup. For the purposes of this game, whenever the answer is to tell your lawyer immediately, that means calling or emailing right away if it's during business hours. If it's after business hours, you shouldn't call her at home or on her mobile phone (unless your lawyer has specifically told you to do so). If there's ever an immediate risk to your children's or your safety, you should call 911 first, not your lawyer.

Scenario 1. Your friend tells you she saw your ex and a blonde half his age—both in yoga attire—leaving a yoga studio and getting into his car.

Answer. This is one for your BFF and maybe your therapist. At most, you may decide to include it on the weekly roundup, but you don't need to call your lawyer right away.

Scenario 2. You are so depressed, you called in sick at work two days in a row.

Answer. Call your therapist and your BFF. This is not a matter for your lawyer. But if you are in a custody battle and you're unable to get out of bed when your kids are at your house, you should put this on the weekly roundup because your ability to properly care for your kids may get called into question by your ex and his lawyer. You don't want your lawyer to get blindsided by this.

Scenario 3. Your ex dropped off your daughter at your house last night and, once she went inside, he told you he couldn't wait for his lawyer to get you on the witness stand because she is going to rip you to shreds.

Answer. Call your therapist or BFF. Your ex didn't say *he* was going to rip you to shreds; he said his lawyer was going to do that when you're on the witness stand. In other words, it's a euphemism for tough questioning. This statement is immature and uncalled for, but it's not so much a threat as it is divorce tough talk. If your ex says this in front of your daughter, you should put it on the weekly roundup because that would be inappropriate.

Scenario 4. Your kids tell you they don't want to go to their dad's house this coming weekend.

Answer. This is one for your BFF and your kids' counselor if they have one. This is a garden-variety kid complaint during a divorce. Unless your kids have told you something that makes you concerned for their safety or well-being while at their dad's house (he drinks until he passes out, he has creepy friends hanging around, or he's verbally or physically abusive), there is no need to tell your lawyer.

Scenario 5. You checked your bank account balances online and noticed your savings account had been zeroed out.

Answer. Tell your lawyer immediately. Financial matters like these require quick and decisive legal action.

Scenario 6. Your ex came over to your house with a listing agreement for your lake house and demanded that you sign it.

Answer. Tell your lawyer immediately. If your ex simply emailed you to say he thinks selling the lake house would be a good idea, reply by telling him that all communications on matters like that need to go through your lawyer and then forward the email to her.

Scenario 7. You stumbled across a secret email account that your ex had been using to communicate with call girls. The email correspondence makes clear that he was hooking up with them while he was away on business trips when you two were still together.

Answer. Tell your lawyer immediately. This information has financial and liability implications. Then talk it over with your therapist and your BFF. Finally, schedule an appointment with your doctor to get tested for STDs.

Scenario 8. When your ex dropped your kids off at your house, he screamed that you were a [bleeping] bitch and that you were going to be left penniless when he was through with you, and he threatened to take away the kids, too. Then he threw your son's backpack on the ground and peeled off. All this was in front of your children and the neighbors.

    Answer. Tell your lawyer immediately. This sort of erratic, belligerent, and threatening behavior is something your lawyer needs to be aware of. Then talk to your therapist and BFF. Plus, tell your kids' therapist about the incident. And if your kids don't have a therapist, consider getting them one. With a dad like that, they're going to need the help.

Scenario 9. An old friend told you recently that one time when she was in town visiting you several years ago, your husband hit on her.

    Answer. This is one for your BFF and maybe your therapist, depending on how much it comes as a surprise to you and whether it bugs you all that much. You could put it on the weekly roundup, too, but it's not all that important.

Scenario 10. Your six-year-old daughter told you that when she spent the night with her dad last weekend, he left her home alone for two hours.

    Answer. Tell your lawyer immediately. Leaving a child that young home alone is a safety issue. You may also want to vent about this to your BFF and therapist. And if your kid has a therapist, this is something to pass along to her, too.

Mind the Store

I know you have a lot on your mind right now, but there are two things you need to put on your "to-do" list when it comes to managing your relationship with your lawyer.

Keep a running log. The next time you're in Target, buy a spiral notebook and keep it handy. Whenever you call your lawyer, jot down the date and time. If you get through to her (or her legal assistant), write down how long your conversation lasted and what the general topic was (i.e., "five minutes: spring break schedule"). When your lawyer calls you, make sure to record the same info. Ditto for texts and emails. This log doesn't need to be a detailed account. The purpose is to help keep things from running together in your mind.

Review your bills. Your lawyer will send you an itemized statement each month detailing the work her office has done on your case. This statement should include a description of the communications she or other people in her office have had with you or anyone else about your divorce, as well as other work they've done on your behalf, such as drafting petitions, agreements, and letters or reviewing documents or correspondence from others. Review your bill each month and cross-check it against your log to make sure it matches up. You don't have to go over the bill with a fine-toothed comb looking for mistakes, but you should read over it to make sure you are aware of what you're being charged for.

Don't Let the Guilt Window Slam Shut (But Don't Fall Out of It Either)

If your divorce is precipitated by a colossal betrayal by your ex (such as an affair that has just come to light), there is often a window of time—I call it the guilt window—when he feels terrible about what he's done. Don't squander this opportunity. Even if you are so stunned by the discovery that you can only think about the betrayal and not the nuts and bolts of your divorce, it behooves you to get the upper hand on your feelings and move quickly to wrap up your divorce. Pull yourself together and do what you can to finalize your divorce before the guilt window closes and he figures out a way to rationalize his behavior.

Conversely, if you're the one who committed the betrayal, don't let your guilty conscience lead you to make bad decisions concerning your property division or custody arrangements. Mommy and Daddy getting a divorce is tough on your kids. Finding out that the divorce was prompted by Mommy's affair can be even tougher. But allowing your guilt to cause you to accept a custody arrangement that gives you a reduced role in your kids' lives or a property settlement that leaves you less able to provide for them can punish them even further. Don't compound the mistakes you've already made by allowing them to motivate you to make brand-new ones.

I'm not saying you don't have to take responsibility for your actions, because you do. That work comes in Part Four, once you're back on your feet. Right now, we're trying to get you off the pavement and keep your kids out of harm's way. To do that, you'll need to separate your past from your present so you can make wise decisions about your future.

Let Your Lawyer Do Her Job

Because this is your personal life, from your standpoint everything that happens regarding you and your ex is relevant to your divorce. But from your lawyer's standpoint, only some of what happens is relevant. That's because your lawyer doesn't take your divorce personally. And although that might initially hit you wrong, it's actually a good thing.

Your lawyer need not be emotionally invested in your divorce to care about you or be conscientious and diligent. Her job is to get your divorce done from a legal and technical standpoint. For her to be able to do that well, her judgment cannot be clouded by emotion.

It's important for you to clearly understand your role when it comes to the legal work involved with getting this deal done. It's your divorce case, but you don't have the lead part. You aren't even the costar. You are a supporting actress: Your part is very important, but to perform it well you can't overact, hog the limelight, or step on other people's lines.

Think of it this way: If you hired a surgeon to operate on your ankle, you wouldn't grab a scalpel and start cutting away alongside her, would you? Of course not. You hired her to do a job because you recognized that you needed the help of a skilled professional. The same is true with your divorce. For your lawyer to do the best job possible, you have to let her handle the things she's supposed to handle, and leave her enough elbow room to do her job.

That means no negotiating deals with your ex behind your lawyer's back. You may think that you will have better luck prevailing upon your ex to be reasonable, but, if you were so good at getting him to be reasonable, chances are you wouldn't be getting a divorce right now. I'm not saying that it's never okay to talk directly with your ex about a deal point; I *am* saying that any strategy to do so should be cleared with your lawyer first. Failure to do so can lead to costly misfires and delays.

If your ex tries to either strong-arm or sweet-talk you into agreeing to something, don't engage. If it's in writing, simply forward it to your lawyer. If he contacts you in person or by phone, tell him that your lawyer is handling the matter for you. And I hope this goes without saying, but you should *never* sign anything that your ex slaps down in front of you, no matter how urgent he insists it is.

Remember who's paying the bills. You're not the lawyer, but you *are* the client and that means there are certain things you have a right to expect. Your lawyer should treat you with respect, keep you informed, explain things to you, respond to your questions in a timely way, and handle your case professionally and responsibly.

The number one complaint I hear from clients about their divorce lawyer is that she doesn't return phone calls or respond to emails promptly. Although it's unreasonable to pepper your lawyer with constant emails, texts, and phone calls, it *is* reasonable to expect timely responses to unneurotic levels of communication. In nonemergency situations a response from your lawyer within two business days is reasonable. There may be times when she can't fully answer your question within that time frame, but in those cases she should let you know why she can't (she's in trial, for example) and when she will be able to get to it.

Don't dillydally. Getting divorced is a team effort. Your lawyer has the lead role, but she cannot do this job without significant help from you. You are in control of all sorts of data and information that she will need at various points along the way; plus, it will be up to you to make certain key decisions. If you do a half-baked job of performing your responsibilities, it will impact how well your lawyer can do her job. If you want your divorce to move along efficiently, it is critical that you respond in a timely manner. If she needs information or a decision, ask her when she needs it and then make sure to meet that deadline.

Also, try to avoid flip-flopping on decisions. Changing your mind can cost you more than just time and money; it can cost you credibility and put your lawyer in a bad position. Take the time you need to think over a matter before you inform your lawyer of your decision, so that you are reasonably sure of your answer. But if despite your best efforts you do end up changing your mind, make sure to inform your lawyer as soon as possible so she can correct course and minimize the collateral damage.

It's not just what you say; it's how you say it. When it comes to communicating with your lawyer, I encourage you to adopt email as your preferred method. Email allows you to take as much time as you need, while the meter is not running, to think through your questions and phrase them clearly and concisely. It also allows you to have your lawyer's answers in a form that permits you to refer to them for free, rather than having to call back and incur more charges. Because your communications with your lawyer are privileged, you don't need to worry about these written Q&As being used against you (unless you do something stupid to waive the privilege, such as forwarding the emails to your ex).

If you let your lawyer know your reasonable preferences and she refuses to accommodate them without offering you an explanation that you find compelling, don't be intimidated. Remember, you are the client and you have a right to have things reasonably tailored to suit you. Think of it this way: What if you ordered a soy latte at Starbucks and the barista responded, "Sorry, that's not the way I make them. I make them with almond milk. They're much better that way."

Would you simply shrug your shoulders and say, "Okay, you're the barista. You know best." Or would you say, "I'm paying for it. I'm going to drink it. I want it with soy milk or I don't want it at all"?

If the barista had said he was out of soy milk, that would be one thing. But simply refusing to accommodate your reasonable request because he prefers making it another way is not acceptable. If you told the barista to heat the milk up an extra ten degrees before frothing it because it froths a lot faster that way, and to use a teaspoon less espresso grounds because it's easier on the machine in the long run, that's a different story. In that scenario you'd be telling the barista how to do his job, rather than telling him your order, and you'd be out of line.

The bottom line is this: Don't be afraid to inform your lawyer of your reasonable preferences, especially those designed to help you manage your communications efficiently and keep the bills down. If she refuses your requests without giving you a reason that makes sense to you, you should consider hiring another lawyer because the one you have is not treating you with basic respect.

Two wrongs don't make a right. If you are unhappy with your lawyer, you should not suffer in silence, but you shouldn't overreact, either. Send her an email explaining your complaints. Be polite, but also be specific:

"On March 4 I emailed you a question about the kids' schedule. It's March 18 and I haven't yet received a response."

Then let her know what you think is reasonable, ask whether she can agree to it, and, if not, what she proposes instead.

"I think getting back to me within two business days is reasonable. I understand you might not always be able to fully answer my question within two days. In those cases I would appreciate your letting me know within that time frame when I can expect a full answer. Is this something you can agree to? And if not, can you let me know what you think is reasonable?"

If you are upset over your bill, use the information from your log to determine whether you are suffering from sticker shock or if there are actual inaccuracies. If the bill matches up with your log of your interactions with your lawyer, that information will at least give you some assurance that your lawyer's timekeeping is accurate. But if the comparison reveals inconsistencies or leaves you with questions, email your lawyer about them. If you haven't discovered any inaccuracies but you are still unhappy with the amount, email your lawyer asking for suggestions on what you both can do to keep the bills down.

Even if your email doesn't result in a downward adjustment to your current bill, it will let your lawyer know that you are detail-oriented and price conscious, and this will help to influence your lawyer's approach to your case in the future. Being clear with your lawyer about your reasonable expectations, reactions, and preferences doesn't make you a bitch; it makes you aboveboard. It's a lot harder for your lawyer to meet your expectations if she doesn't know what they are.

If you follow the advice in this chapter, you will be doing all you can to keep your case moving along while also keeping your legal bills from getting ahead of you. That doesn't mean you won't still suffer from sticker shock from time to time. But when you do, the following classic divorce joke should help you take the long view: Why is divorce so expensive? Because it's worth it.

4.

When Less Really *Is* More
(and Other Valuable Tips for
Communicating with Your Ex)

I like refrigerator magnets with funny sayings on them. Whether they say, "Ran into my ex. Threw it into reverse and hit him again" or "Mommy knows best. That's why she left Daddy," these magnets make me laugh—and laughing is key to staying positive.

When I was going through my divorce, I came across a refrigerator magnet that said, "Please don't interrupt me when I'm ignoring you." I bought this magnet, although I didn't really know why at the time. Then, as my divorce waged on, it became clear. This magnet became my mantra when it came to dealing with my ex. It wasn't that I wanted to snub That Man by giving him the silent treatment, but I needed to remember that the less I communicated with him, the fewer opportunities there would be for our communications to cause additional problems in our divorce. The magnet served as an entertaining reminder of that reality.

Boy, did I need a lot of reminding. My ex had a habit of springing stuff on me and then demanding that I give him an answer (or, worse yet, sign a document) without having a chance to think things over first. This came back to bite me on numerous occasions. For example, one Saturday I was out for a run when he suddenly appeared out of nowhere, running toward me from the opposite direction. He waved me down and I foolishly stopped. He launched into some spiel about how he had gotten an offer on a piece of property that we owned and he wanted my approval to proceed with selling it.

Caught off guard, I stammered that I guess it sounded okay. And voila! Just like that he had a conversation to cite wherein we jointly agreed to sell the piece of property. Never mind that I hadn't known until that moment that he was even trying to sell it, or that I hadn't seen anything in writing, or that I hadn't had a chance to talk the matter over with my lawyer.

I finished my run in a cold sweat, worrying that I had just irreversibly flubbed something up. I went directly home and emailed my lawyer, explaining what had just happened, and spent the rest of the weekend with my stomach in knots. I ended up incurring extra attorney's fees to straighten out a mess that would have never happened had I declined to stop and talk to my ex that day, or if I had simply said he needed to run that question through the lawyers.

But something positive did come from my mistakes. I developed some solid guidelines to follow when it comes to communicating with your ex during your divorce, so you don't have to learn these lessons the hard way.

He's Your Ex, Not Your Best Friend

The number one thing to remember when you are communicating with your ex is to keep it short and sweet. And if you can't do both, keep it even shorter. You may be one of those rare people who is on good terms with your ex, but, if getting a divorce teaches you anything, it's that feelings can change. The fact that you are getting along now doesn't mean you will continue to get along in the future. What's more, getting along well with your ex during your divorce can actually put you at risk. That's because the frequent communications that often go hand in hand with a friendly relationship can lead to sharing too much information—about your current activities, your future plans, and what's most important to you. Then, if you reach a point at which things aren't so friendly between the two of you, he has information that could be used against you.

However close you may feel to him and however well you might be getting along at the moment, the two of you are currently on opposite sides of a lawsuit. That doesn't mean you have to hate each other, but that does mean you have opposing interests, whether or not you want to see it that way. If your divorce negotiations get contentious or if one of you gets angry at the other, you could easily end up regretting all the sharing you did when you were getting along well.

Think of it like this: If you are trying to buy a house, there are things you should not share with the seller no matter how friendly you feel toward him. These things would include the maximum amount you'd be willing to pay for the house, whether you have certain time limitations that the seller could possibly exploit, or that you have your heart set on this specific house. You may genuinely like your seller, but you should never lose sight of the fact that you two are on opposite sides of the table when it comes to the transaction.

The same is true with your ex and your divorce. If you and your ex are getting along well, congratulations to both of you. But remember, while your divorce is pending, there can definitely be too much of a good thing. Feel free to enjoy the friendly tone, but be careful not to share too much.

Communicate Only When Necessary

The less you communicate with your ex, the fewer opportunities there will be for drama. Even conversations that start off as friendly banter can end up going off the rails without you even realizing what's happening. Then, before you know it, your day is wrecked and your lawyers have another matter to sort out. It's fine to greet your ex when you have a face-to-face encounter, but you should be wary of any conversation beyond a simple exchange of pleasantries.

Spoken conversations are often communication minefields. Subtle things like tone of voice, pregnant pauses, and off-the-cuff quips can cause a conversation to erupt into an argument before you know it. Unless you are recording the call (which you should not do unless your lawyer has advised you otherwise), having a conversation with your ex leaves you with no record of what was actually said (or not said). If he claims you said things you didn't, you have no way of disproving it. This leaves the door wide open for a huge "he said, she said" fight, and that can raise both tensions and legal bills.

When you must talk to your ex face-to-face or on the telephone, assume that your ex is wearing a wire and the judge and jury are sitting in an unmarked van parked outside your house, listening in. Make sure you keep it brief and cordial.

Another bad way to communicate is through text messages. Sure, they provide you with a written record. But most people fire off texts without giving proper consideration to what they've written, and that means they end up with the worst of both worlds: You say impulsive things *and* you put them in writing. That's a lose-lose scenario.

Because you are represented by counsel, there's no need to discuss any matter with your ex that's being handled by your attorney. After all, that's why you are paying her. If you commission someone to paint a portrait of your children, you wouldn't pick up a paintbrush and start painting alongside her. Why? Because your efforts would slow the work down, the artist would have to fix your mistakes, and the final product would be worse as a result. The same thing goes for involving yourself in matters that your lawyer is handling. Not only will your meddling not help things along, but it is likely to impede progress, if not derail it altogether.

So, if your ex tries to initiate a conversation about topics that are being handled by your lawyer, do not take the bait. If the attempt is face-to-face or by phone, tell him that any discussion of the matter needs to go through your lawyer. If the attempt is by email, reply that your lawyer is handling the matter and all correspondence should be directed to her, and then forward the email to your lawyer. If he persists, do not reply but be sure to reference the additional emails on your weekly roundup to your lawyer. If your ex sends you any emails that you feel are inappropriate or make you uncomfortable, do not engage. Forward them to your lawyer instead. If your ex leaves you voice mails that are inappropriate, make sure to save them and forward them to your lawyer.

Tips to Follow When Communicating Is a Must

When you can choose how to deliver a message, the best method is by email, provided you are savvy enough to both avail yourself of the advantages and sidestep the disadvantages. Email gives you the opportunity to carefully consider what you want to say while also affording your ex the chance to process the information without being put on the spot. Email also provides you with a written record of what was said, which can be a blessing or a curse depending on how much intelligence and self-control you have. To make sure you get the most out of your correspondence with your ex, stick to the following guidelines:

Click it forward. Let's say you get an email on Tuesday from your six-year-old daughter Becca's soccer coach telling you that a makeup soccer game has been scheduled for Thursday at 4:00 PM. Restating the information in a new email has no upside. Once you start writing, you might end up with this before you know it:

> *You may have forgotten this since you were hardly ever home before we split up, but you have a six-year-old daughter and her name is Becca. She likes soccer*

and plays on a team. Coach Kyle emailed to say there is a makeup game this Thursday at 4:00 PM. Normally, I wouldn't expect you to have any interest in going, since you never bothered to come to any of her games before. But now that we are getting a divorce and you are suddenly acting like you are running for Father of the Year, I realize this might be of interest to you, especially because there will be a crowd of other parents there for you to try to impress. Since this game is on a day that Becca is with you, you will be responsible for getting her to and from the game. Also, Becca will need a snack and a water bottle, so don't forget to ask either your secretary or your new girlfriend to take care of those things for you.

As satisfying as it may be to write this email, sending it would not be worth the consequences. Not only could the blowback from it end up costing you thousands of extra dollars in attorney's fees, but it would be absolutely no fun to have to read that out loud in court.

A better approach is simply to forward the email to your ex with a simple "See below" or "FYI" preface. Forwarding the message without restating or adding anything substantive avoids the risk of getting something wrong, leaving something out, adding in some tone, or being accused of trying to act as gatekeeper of the information. You can dodge all of those bullets by simply hitting the forward button instead.

Stick to the facts. For the times when you can't simply hit forward, a good way to ensure that your email contains only relevant information is to use bullet-point formatting. Your email should answer the questions who, what, where, and when, but not why or how. When you get into why and how, you risk letting tone sneak in.

In the example about Becca's makeup soccer game, imagine that instead of getting an email, you get a voicemail from her coach. At your earliest opportunity, you should send your ex an email that says the following:

- Who and What: Becca has a makeup soccer game.
- When: Thursday at 4:00 PM.
- Where: City Park.
- For more information, call Coach Kyle.

There is nothing in that email that has any hint of attitude. It simply and efficiently passes on information.

Be timely. If you get an email that your ex needs to see, don't sit on the information and send it at the last minute. It doesn't take much for your ex and his lawyer to connect the dots between when you got word of something and when you got around to passing the information on. If the information that you sat on had to do with schedule items for your kids, that kind of gamesmanship puts you in a terrible light. The last thing you need right now is to incur extra attorney's fees trying to explain why you were being manipulative. Be both wise and mature, and hit the forward button as soon as you get it.

Don't send emails at crazy o'clock. No matter how reasonable the content may be, nothing says crazy like sending an email to your ex at 2:00 AM. It could be something as mundane as a reminder about school photo day, but, if it's sent in the middle of the night, it makes you look off-kilter. The truth is, you are less likely to have clear judgment if you are awake when you should be asleep.

Even if your email checks out perfectly, the timestamp tells him that in the middle of the night you were (a) not sleeping and (b) writing him an email. That's definitely more information than he needs to know about you. Adopt a strict policy of not sending any emails to your ex after 10:00 PM or before 7:00 AM. If you do draft an email after 10:00 PM, save it as a draft and send it in the morning—after you've proofread it one last time.

Be a draft dodger. Another excellent way to dodge bullets is by writing a draft first. If the information you are conveying is not time sensitive, take your time. Write out what you want to say and don't look at it again until the next day. Then put yourself in the position of your ex and read it all the way through, carefully checking for tone. Your goal should be to have an email that is both cordial and contains 100 percent information and zero percent personality. Personality involves attitude and tone, and attitude and tone get you into trouble.

Then cross-check it another way by reading it out loud while pretending that you are in front of a judge and jury. How do you think the email makes you sound? Bitchy? Micromanaging? Spiteful? Bitter? Crazy? Imagine if your boss were to come across this communication. Does the thought of her reading it embarrass you? If so, why? Is it the tone or the entire subject matter?

Finally, if the message is not time sensitive and it's not about the kids' schedule, you should ask yourself if it's really necessary at all, and then think long and hard before sending it. Unless your email passes all of those tests, do not hit the send button.

Safety guaranteed. Whenever you're drafting an email to your ex, safeguard against misfires by inserting your own email address, rather than his, in the "to" space until you are absolutely, positively ready to send it. If you write the email and then decide against sending it, don't be frustrated with yourself for having wasted the time to begin with. Be proud of yourself for having exercised restraint in the end. Consider it a therapeutic exercise that helped you to process your thoughts and feelings while still respecting the all-important principle of keeping communication with your ex to an absolute minimum.

Your Ex Is the Home Depot Guy

One of the biggest risks of communicating with your ex is the negative effect it can have on your mood. One cheap shot from him can suck you straight into the divortex, where you'll find yourself getting whipped around like Sandra Bullock in *Gravity* while you obsess over every detail of your divorce. But you can't just give your ex the silent treatment when you're dropping off or picking up your kids, because that would be weird and unhealthy. You have to be able to see him and make small talk without it messing with your head and undoing your forward momentum.

Home Depot man to the rescue! When you go to Home Depot and you need help carrying something to your car, who helps you? The Home Depot man. And when the Home Depot man is helping you, what do you do? You are pleasant—not because you genuinely like him, but because you are a decent person. You greet him. You may exchange some pleasantries while you walk to the car. After he loads the item in the trunk, you thank him for his help.

What happens after that? You close the trunk, get in your car, and drive off. And here's the best part: You don't give the Home Depot man another thought. You think about what you're going to have for dinner, or your current project at work, or your next errand, or what time you need to pick up your kids, or a million other things. But you don't think about the Home Depot man.

Your ex is the Home Depot man. When you see him, be minimally polite. Don't bring up or get tricked into talking to him about anything personal. That would be inappropriate; after all, he's the Home Depot man. Limit your conversation to a superficial exchange of pleasantries. Then, when the exchange is over, don't waste your time analyzing every word he said. Don't mull over what he *really* meant when he said, "Have a nice weekend." Don't wonder if he's seeing anyone. Don't try to figure out whether he's talked to any of your friends. As soon as you're done with the minimal exchange, don't give it another thought. Move on to thinking about something or someone that actually matters in your life.

Your thoughts and emotional energy are your most valuable resources right now—more valuable than cold, hard cash. Just as you wouldn't willingly fork over a pile of money to your ex right now, you shouldn't give him a chunk of the precious space inside your head, either. Whenever you find yourself thinking about your ex, mentally put him in a bright orange Home Depot apron. That should put him in his place.

PART TWO:

SECURE YOUR OWN MASK FIRST

5.

Taking Care of Number One

Let's play a quick game of make-believe. Ready? Imagine it's the end of May and your son is preparing for finals. (If you don't have any kids, instead imagine your best friend or sister in a similarly intense situation.) He's in his junior year of high school, so these exams count for a lot. These will be the last grades on his transcript that will accompany his college applications. He has his heart set on getting into a certain college, and it's a tough one to get into. In other words, it's crunch time for him. This is the biggest thing he's faced in his life so far, and a lot is riding on it. It's a one-shot deal with no do-overs.

As the mom of this kid, how would you support him during this stressful time? Would you ride him about his chores or ease up on him in light of the circumstances? If you noticed that he looked a little disheveled at breakfast, would you pester him about his appearance or let it go? If you saw him heading to his room with a bag of Cheetos, would you gripe at him about his nutrition or skip the lecture this time?

My guess is this: You would pick up his slack when it comes to his normal household responsibilities, such as taking out the trash or emptying the dishwasher. I bet you'd even bus his dishes for him. If you noticed he looked a little rumpled, you'd probably let it go. I'm also willing to bet the whole thing with the Cheetos would have never happened because you would have offered to make him a healthy snack before he got that desperate. You wouldn't worry for an instant about all of this spoiling him, because you know he's behind the eight ball. And when someone you love is behind the eight ball, you tend to pitch in and give him some extra love and support.

Of course, if your son were playing video games all night long and not studying at all, your approach would be totally different. You'd likely crack the whip over him and bring pressure to bear wherever and however necessary. But when he is trying his best in the face of a big challenge, your response is to do what you can to help him succeed.

Here's the thing: You occupy both sides of that equation right now. You are that kid at the moment. And you are also that kid's mom. What does that mean? It means you have to be as understanding and supportive of yourself as possible during your divorce because it is going to take all your strength and energy to get through it.

You know how flight attendants instruct you to secure your own mask first before helping children with theirs? The same logic applies when you're getting a divorce. You have to make sure your oxygen supply is in place in order to get through this ordeal and to be in a position to help your children. And your kids are going to need a lot of help right now, so it's more important than ever to maintain your health.

This is one of the biggest challenges you've faced in your life and there is a tremendous amount at stake. You are going to be stressed out, exhausted, and emotionally drained. Right now, simply making it through each day is a huge accomplishment. You have to make a conscious, consistent effort to put one foot in front of the other while you head in the right direction. Taking excellent care of yourself is a must. You also have to know when to cut yourself a break or two.

What makes this stretch so daunting is that on top of the emotional trauma caused by your marriage coming to an end, a big chunk of your identity and your entire routine has been thrown out the window, so you cannot even take comfort in your sense of self and the rhythm of your everyday life. All of this creates a triple whammy that can throw you into emotional shock. When you're in emotional shock, it helps to have some clear steps to follow rather than abstract advice.

Use the following list of "dos and don'ts" both as a guide to help you get through each day and as a starting point to create a framework for your new everyday life. As time goes by, you can customize this routine so it becomes more and more your own.

The Dos

Eat right. The weight you've dropped since the divorce bomb detonated is not an indication of healthy living; it's evidence of extreme stress. Don't let the fact that you can get away with eating anything you want right now without gaining any weight distract you from what your body really needs: healthy fuel. Stress wreaks havoc on you both emotionally and physically. Make sure you're eating nutritious food to replenish and sustain your body while you endure these extreme conditions. Fill your diet with whole grains, plenty of fresh fruit and vegetables, raw nuts, legumes, and lean protein. Your focus should be on quality, not calories.

If you've been gaining weight during this period, the same principle applies. If you tend to be an emotional eater, don't use food as a way to self-medicate; use it as a way to heal. If you haven't been coached on what constitutes good nutrition, now is a perfect time to read about that or even sign up for a class.

Hydrate. Water is good for you. So drink up. It will help you to both look and feel better—from improving your skin to brightening your bloodshot eyes. Have as many rounds of water as you want, but be careful not to drink too much too close to bedtime. You don't want the need for frequent trips to the bathroom to wake you at a time when it might be difficult to fall back to sleep.

Get physical. Make exercise part of your everyday life. The point of exercising right now isn't to tone up your body; it's to de-stress your mind. Exercise is one of the best ways to offload stress and fight depression. Plus, getting regular exercise will help you to sleep better. Finally, since you are in the process of constructing a new normal, it's the perfect time to fold daily exercise into your regular routine.

Keep calm. Make a point to prioritize any activity that gives you a sense of calm. If you find comfort in organized religion, be religious about going to church on Sundays. Have more of an Eastern sensibility? Even if you're not feeling all that peaceful right now, yoga and meditation can keep you zen-tered until you find your bliss again. In a twelve-step program? Now's the time to step up your meetings. If reading is your road map to calm, get lost in a book for a little while each day. The point is to figure out what gives you a sense of balance, and make room for that in your daily schedule.

Sleep it off. There's nothing like a divorce to wreck your ability to get a good night's sleep. And getting enough sleep is critical to being able to function and make good decisions. The following measures can help maximize your chances of getting as much quality sleep as possible: Try to get to bed at about the same time each night. Bodies like routines, and getting into bed at a regular time each night will help train yours to recognize which hours are for sleeping. Studies show that working on your laptop and watching TV too close to bedtime can interfere with falling asleep. So, power down by reading a book instead. Finally, resist the urge to check your phone if you wake up in the middle of the night. Either keep it facedown on your nightstand or consider leaving it in another room altogether.

The Don'ts

Don't beat yourself up. Every last one of us who has gotten a divorce has some responsibility for the demise of our relationship. Why? Because no one is perfect. But there are real regrets and then there are counterfeit ones. It's important to be able to distinguish between the two, because what you do with each of them is very different. You need to make sure you don't get tricked into spending any of your precious resources beating yourself up over the worthless ones.

Examples of real regrets include being emotionally unavailable, being consumed with your career or your kids (or both) to the point where you ignored your spouse and allowed your relationship to fall to the very last place on your list of priorities, engaging in an emotional and/or physical affair, becoming a controlling shrew or a relentless nag, or even picking a jerk for a husband and then not having the backbone to call him on his nonsense.

Examining any real regrets so you can take responsibility for your missteps and misdeeds is as painful as it is necessary. No divorce recovery is complete without it. And there will come a time when we take that step together. But it's too soon. Trying to do that at this stage would be like trying to play tennis with a broken wrist. Right now, our work is to get you up off the ground, bandage up your wounds, help you to regain your strength and balance, and teach you how to stand on your own two feet again. Once we've accomplished all that, then it will be time to look at these real regrets so we can figure out what you need to learn from them before they are permanently warehoused.

Examples of counterfeit regrets include thinking that you should have worn sexier lingerie to bed every night, or you should have spent less on music lessons and braces for the kids and more on Botox and microdermabrasion for yourself, or you should have bought all your clothes at Forever 21 even though it's been forever since you were actually twenty-one. In other words, counterfeit regrets involve telling yourself if only you had been prettier, younger, hotter, or more bubbly and attentive, then he wouldn't have had an affair with his hot young administrative assistant and your marriage wouldn't be coming to an end.

If you find yourself mired in counterfeit regret over things like the kind of jammies you wore to bed each night, the first thing to remember is this: You wore the kind of jammies that enabled you to get out of bed and run to your kids' rooms if they woke up suddenly with a nightmare or the stomach flu. Then ask yourself: What was your ex wearing to bed each night? Those ratty boxers with the Christmas motif he got at Old Navy a thousand years ago? Do you think he's spent one second feeling bad about what he wore to bed? And if your divorce was precipitated by his affair, do you think he's felt any remorse over stealing time, energy, and money from you and your family, and squandering them on his outside love interest?

That's the danger of counterfeit regrets. They sneak into your head and do this Jedi mind trick on you so that you take responsibility not only for your own errors or omissions but your ex's, too. When you blame yourself for acting and dressing your age and otherwise being yourself, you become an unwitting participant in what is already a pile-on for your flattened self-esteem.

You trusted that you and your husband were both playing by the same rules. You thought you were both equally dedicated to putting your family first. If he had an affair, it is not your fault that he deceived you and failed to keep his word, while you kept yours. Whatever your mistakes may have been, you are not also responsible for his, no matter what you were or were not wearing at any given moment.

Stewing over the counterfeit regrets is tantamount to beating yourself up. And beating yourself up is not helpful—not now, not later, not ever. Not only does it keep you from moving forward, but it can actually push you backward. So, when you find yourself blaming yourself for all errors, omissions, and betrayals—his and yours—redirect your thoughts to what you need to be working on right now: taking care of yourself so you can get through the day.

Don't lean on crutches. There are healthy and unhealthy ways of dealing with stress. Healthy ways fortify you; unhealthy ways weaken you. For example, crunches help you blow off steam and result in a stronger you, but crutches only medicate away your worries. When the medication wears off, you're left with the same list of troubles—plus a new one: a possible dependency. With that in mind, make sure you don't drink too much alcohol during this stretch. It's not necessary to be a teetotaler (unless you are an alcoholic, of course), but make moderation your mantra.

That goes for coffee, too. Some coffee is fine. But too much coffee can interfere with sleep and that can make your situation worse. Even things that are generally good for you, such as sleeping and eating, can be overdone to the point of becoming a crutch. And keep this in mind: Just because you can get a prescription for a sleep aid or a mood adjuster doesn't mean you should take it. Before resorting to a pharmaceutical solution, make sure you're doing all you can to facilitate sleep, stabilize your mood, and get rid of stress.

Don't date. Dating requires an output of time and energy—two precious resources you cannot afford to give away right now. All of your energy should be committed to one thing: getting you and your kids through this transition. You may be thinking that dating would actually help you because a little attention from the opposite sex would serve as balm for your battered self-esteem. But that mind-set reveals that you are looking to date as a way to self-medicate, and that means you are far from ready to dive back into the dating pool.

Healthy dating requires both giving and taking. You're not in a position to give, so it's not fair to take. Between getting divorced and taking good care of your kids, your plate is full. There will be plenty of time to date later—when your divorce is final, you and your kids have adjusted to your new normal life, and you've had time to perform an autopsy on your marriage to determine the exact cause of death.

If all that isn't enough to convince you to hold off, consider this: There's nothing like dating before your divorce is final to turn an unpleasant divorce into a bloodbath of epic proportions. The introduction of a new love interest often injects pain, jealousy, competitiveness, and insecurity into an already volatile mix. When this happens, your ex's goal becomes exacting revenge or otherwise getting back at you rather than simply getting the divorce done. Oftentimes this goal is subconscious, making it impossible for anyone to challenge with reason or logic. Whenever you have the chance, you should choose to keep things as simple as possible. This is one of those times. Make the right choice.

Don't overspend. Establishing a new life can be expensive. It takes a lot of money to set up a new household and pay for lawyers and therapists. That's a lot of additional costs to cover on a budget that previously supported only one household. Be careful not to further stress your bottom line by piling on additional unnecessary discretionary expenses. Remember your judgment is not the best right now. So, if you find yourself going on weekend

shopping sprees or booking dream vacations, drop your smol-
dering credit card and back away slowly with your hands in
plain sight. Whether or not you are accustomed to this kind of
spending, continuing to shop 'til you drop can jeopardize both
the outcome of your divorce as well as your ability to start fresh.
There's nothing like a mountain of consumer debt to hamstring
your effort to turn the page and start a new chapter.

6.

Nobody Puts Baby in the Middle

When it comes to cutting people off at the knees, divorce does not engage in age discrimination. It is an equal opportunity assaulter. You may feel as if you're riding shotgun in a car that just careened over the guardrail and is now free-falling toward the jagged rocks below. As helpless as that feels, it's likely your kids feel even worse. Why? Because they have even less control over this situation than you.

From their standpoint, their world has been completely shaken up. Bits and pieces of their everyday life are now swirling around them like a Hiroshima snow globe and they have no idea where everything will land. Where will their parents live? Will either one move out of town? Whom will they live with? Will *they* have to move out of town? Will brothers and sisters get separated? Where will the family pets live? Will they have to move away from their friends? Will they have to change schools? Will both parents be okay? Will they be poor now? Will Mom quit crying? Will Dad stop acting like an overgrown adolescent? Will anything ever seem normal again?

In case you're thinking that your own list of questions is pretty much the same, there is one huge difference in your respective situations: You are a grownup and they are kids. More important, you are the parent and they are your children. Whether or not you wanted this divorce, you are on the front lines of it, for better or for worse (pardon the pun). Although that means you stand to take most of the incoming fire, it also means you have a say over your side's battle plans.

Your kids, on the other hand, are simply caught in the crossfire of a war they didn't start, can't stop, and have no control over. And on top of all that, they see their parents—the two people who are supposed to keep them safe and provide a stable home—coming unglued. Now *that's* terrifying.

So, what does this mean for you? In Chapter Five, we talked about the concept of securing your own mask first before helping others with theirs, just as you do when you fly. We also discussed how that means doing whatever is in your power to ensure that you are as healthy as possible so you can meet your responsibilities to the best of your ability under very difficult circumstances. If you have children still living at home, your number one responsibility is shepherding your kids through your divorce while shielding them from as much of the toxic fallout as possible.

If you think this sounds too overwhelming for you to take on right now, I have two responses for you—one "nicey-nice" and the other "tough love." Let's get the "tough love" one out of the way first. I have three words for you: Suck it up. Look, we're talking about your kids here. They are hurting, scared, and maybe angry—all because of their parents' inability to make the very endeavor that gave rise to their existence, the marriage, work. So, whether or not you think you have the energy to take this on right now, it's on anyway. Plenty of times, parents have to tell kids they don't have a choice when it comes to doing something they don't want to do, such as homework or chores. This time, it's your turn to get that message.

Now for the "nicey-nice" response: You may think you don't have the energy to help your children right now. But I'm here to tell you that as much as your kids need you to do this for them, this is also going to be really good for you. One key to getting through this divorce is putting one foot in front of the other until your life begins to take shape again. Staying busy takes conscious effort. You need to fill your time with activities that are healthy and constructive. And orbiting around in the divortex, obsessing over your ex and/or your divorce, doesn't count as either. Some amount of busywork is fine, but substantive and important projects are good, too. And no project is more substantive and important than shepherding your kids through your divorce.

So, it's all settled. You're going to do this and you're going to do this well. And I will help you. Let's go over the rules that will ensure that, when this is all over, you'll look back on the job you did and feel proud.

You Don't Get a Time-Out from Being a Mom

There are things you need to do (or not do) to maintain a healthy relationship with your kids and provide a positive home life for them, and then there are things you need to do (or not do) to avoid interfering with your kids' chances of having a healthy relationship with their dad. Let's cover them in that order.

Don't divorce your kids. Whether you are devastated over this divorce or feel that you've just been sprung from prison, abandoning your kids is not an option. You're divorcing your husband, not your children. Yes, one chapter of your life is ending and another is beginning, and that gives you great leeway to decide how to redefine who you are, but you don't get to redefine yourself to the point where you renege on your commitment to raise your children.

That means you can't move out of town, leaving them behind. And you can't just leave your ex holding the bag when it comes to raising them, even if you feel you have single-handedly raised them with no help from him until this point. Nor can you pawn them off on other people or leave them in front of the television with a bowl of Kraft Macaroni & Cheese while you hit the bars with your BFFs.

When your kids move away for college, then you can follow your bliss. But now more than ever, they need all the stability and love they can get. If you take only one thing away from this book, it should be this: Don't bail on your kids during (or after) your divorce. That is the single most important piece of advice I have to give you.

Being sad is okay; being nonfunctional isn't. When you're going through something as difficult as divorce, being sad is to be expected. It's okay—even good, arguably—for your kids to pick up on the fact that you're sad or worried sometimes, or even to stumble across you crying occasionally. After all, you and their dad are getting divorced and that's a big deal.

But it's not okay for them to see you refuse to get out of bed on a weekday morning to help them get ready for school. It's super uncool for them to come home from school and find you still in bed, not showered, rocking the same boxers and T-shirt you've had on for three days straight. And it's completely unacceptable for your kids to see you hitting the bottle or turning to other substances, or other men, to medicate your way through this crisis.

Regardless of how much you're hurting, you owe it to your kids to keep functioning as a healthy human being. You do not have exclusive ownership of this crisis. They are all caught up in it, too—and they need a mom with her act together to help them through it.

Here's a sobering thought: They are learning how to handle tough situations when they're grownups from watching you right now. If you don't want them to be catatonic or self-destructive when life punches them in the gut, then model a better way. They're taking notes, so be a good teacher.

Make your house a home. Whether you've moved to a new place or your ex has gotten a place of his own, your kids need your house to feel like home. If you are moving, make sure to get a place that has enough bedrooms to accommodate your kids. I'm not saying each kid has to have his own room; I'm only saying that there has to be at least a bedroom for daughters and a bedroom for sons, and those rooms need to be separate from your bedroom and also not double as the living room or your office.

Moving to a place that does not have room for your kids is not viewed favorably by judges and juries, and sends your kids the message that you are downsizing them out of your home. A bedroom in your house is an important physical message that your kids always have a place in your life.

Next, make sure to unpack everything, hang familiar things on the walls, and put out family photos. Even though the living space might be new, your goal should be to make it feel homey and give it an air of familiarity.

If your ex has moved out, make sure to rearrange the furniture enough to eliminate any gaping holes left by things he has taken. Don't rearrange everything—that can be unsettling to your kids. But if your ex took the couch and the coffee table, go buy a new couch and coffee table. If that's not in the budget, get secondhand ones at a garage sale or from a friend, or move the chairs and end tables around to fill in the space. Before long your kids' eyes will adjust to the new look of the living room.

Get a counselor to help your kids. If your kids are struggling with the split and you are concerned about how to handle it, set them up with a counselor who specializes in helping children through this type of transition. But don't assume that all counselors are equal. As with lawyers, reputation, personality, and style matter. To be effective, the counselor needs to be a good match for your kids.

Don't use your kids as your BFFs. Sometimes, certain kids—often the older ones—want to play the role of confidant or even protector. Daughters may want to stroke your hair and rub your shoulders when you are sad. Sons may want to act like the new "man of the house." And you may be tempted to let them. Having them in that role feels good because it creates a feeling of closeness, and not letting them play that role might make you feel that you're rebuffing them or shutting them out.

But don't be fooled by those feelings. By not allowing your kids to prop you up emotionally, what you're really doing is being a responsible parent and protecting them. You're protecting their childhood, protecting their role as kids, protecting your authority as parent, and protecting their relationship with their dad. Even if you don't have any interest in that last one for your ex's sake, you should for your kids' sake.

When you put kids in the position of being your confidant or protector, it reverses the role of parent and child—caregiver and care receiver—which isn't good for your relationship in the long run. And even if you're careful not to trash-talk their dad in the process, it still undermines their relationship with him.

Being your confidant while you're hurting can make your children resent the source of your pain: their dad. They may grow reluctant to spend time with him because they feel like they're betraying you when they do, and they think they need to be home to keep you from falling apart. All this puts your kids in a position of having too much responsibility for your emotional well-being. So, lean on the members of your A-Team for emotional support (Chapter Seven explains what this is and how to set yours up), and make sure your kids know they get to lean on you rather than the other way around.

Don't date until your divorce is final. I know I've said this before, but it definitely bears repeating: Dating before your divorce is final is a bad idea. There is a zero percent chance that dating will make your divorce go more smoothly. There's a bazillion percent chance it will increase the drama, which will in turn make your divorce take longer and cost more. Plus, it robs you of the chance to figure out your share of the responsibility for why your marriage didn't work out so you can have a realistic chance at getting it right the next time you enter into a relationship.

On top of all that, here's another really big reason not to date before your divorce is final: It's not good for your kids. They need to process the change in the family structure and the loss of living in a two-parent household. They need to come to terms with the fact that their mom and dad aren't going to be together anymore. Respect your kids' need to sort through this by giving them the time to do it. You'll also be modeling responsible adult behavior by not getting out of one relationship and immediately jumping into another.

If you need a selfish reason to wait, consider this: Your kids are more likely to accept a subsequent relationship if they don't feel you're betraying their dad or abandoning them. When you rush into another relationship too fast, they may end up feeling that you're doing both. Assuming you follow the advice in this book, your divorce will be final soon enough and there will be plenty of time to date in the future.

If delayed gratification just isn't your thing and you simply cannot wait until the wreckage from your marriage is towed away before plowing into your next relationship, at least have the good sense to keep your kids out of it. They have enough to deal with right now, so don't add to their emotional chaos by introducing them to your next Mr. Wrong.

Assuming your kids spend time with their dad, the upside to this arrangement is that it gives you the chance to have some personal time. Schedule your dates during the days when your kids are with their dad. And when they're with you, make them your priority.

You Don't Get a Do-Over on Picking Their Dad

Now, let's talk about what you need to do (or not do) to avoid interfering with your kids' relationship with their dad. Your kids didn't choose their dad; you did. And they can't divorce their dad, but you can. So, unless he's actively abusing drugs, alcohol, or them, your kids will be better off now and in the long run if they have a relationship with him.

Root for your ex to be a good dad. Think of it this way: Singing and dancing are two distinct talents. Someone can be a terrible singer, but a good dancer—and vice versa. The same thing is true when it comes to being a spouse and parent. So, if you're secretly thinking that, if your ex is a bad dad, it will somehow reinforce to everyone that he is also a jerky ex—or if he is a good dad, people will think he was less of a jackass to you—the temporary insanity that comes with a nasty divorce is clouding your logic. If your ex is a tool to you, you should hope and pray that, although you may have chosen a sorry guy to be your husband, at least you didn't saddle your kids with a bad dad, too. Your ex being a better dad than he was a husband—or ex-husband—will actually help you look better.

Also, don't assume that just because he was "hands off" or AWOL while you were married, he will be the same kind of dad after you split up. There's nothing like a custody battle to make a dad suddenly start acting as if he's running for Father of the Year. Watching this can make you crazy, I know. All the years when you were married, he couldn't be bothered to put down the TV remote and play with the kids, he never had time to go to school meetings, and he had no idea what their pediatrician's name was. Now he's posting photos on Facebook of all the adorable moments they're sharing, signing up to be room parent, and scheduling their teeth cleanings.

You'll feel like making snarky comments about how radically different his parenting is now that the divorce (or his divorce lawyer) has caused him to find his Parenting Jesus. And I don't doubt it when you say his newfound attachment to his children is either just for show or simply motivated by a desire to win them like the other property that's up for grabs in the divorce. But these are things you point out to your lawyer (once), and then complain about to your A-Team once you've manned it.

At the end of the day, even if his motivation for being a better dad is a bad one, your kids stand to benefit from his new behavior. And cutting him down to your kids not only hurts them but also can hurt your position in the custody battle, because now you're alienating their affection for him. Not smart.

The bottom line is this: Rooting for your ex to be a good dad means you are rooting for your kids, and rooting for him to be a bad dad means you are rooting against your kids. Be the kind of mom who roots for her kids.

Don't engineer your ex's disappearance from your kids' lives. Trust me, I get it. You wish you never had to see this man again as long as you live. But since you had kids with him—and that was your choice, not theirs—you owe it to them not to get in the way of their chance to have a decent relationship with their dad.

Some moms either subconsciously or intentionally make it so difficult for their ex to maintain a relationship with their kids that he eventually gives up and drifts away. You don't want your children to later wrestle with abandonment issues because you made their dad feel that it was impossible to carry on with visitation. I'm not saying you should be a doormat or put up with unreasonable treatment. And you don't have to pretend he's your best friend. But you have to keep your own emotions out of it and treat him with basic decency when it comes to his role as your kids' father. That means don't make drop-offs and pickups feel like drama-fests or the next ice age. Remember what we talked about in Chapter Four: Treat your ex like the Home Depot man. Nothing more. Nothing less.

Don't trash-talk their dad. In cases in which your ex has been terrible to you, this can be really hard. Believe me, I know. As I said before, your ex can be a decent (or even good) dad, even if he was a terrible husband and is acting like a complete tool during your divorce. In the end, you should want that for your kids.

This doesn't mean you have to cover up his jerky behavior. Say, for example, in an attempt to get his way on an unrelated issue, he refuses to sign the kids' passport renewal applications and that in turn blows your summer vacation plans. It's fair to say to them, "Sorry, kids, but without your dad's signature we can't renew your passports, and without passports we can't go to Costa Rica. Let's pick another vacation spot that doesn't require passports."

But it's not okay to add, "This is just like him. He has always been such a tyrant. He'll do anything to get his way, no matter whom he screws over. This reminds me of another time he was a total jerk to me. . . ." To the extent that their dad has flaws, your kids will discover them for themselves over time. They do not need you highlighting all his shortcomings for them.

You shouldn't trash your ex to your kids, but you don't have to pretend that you think he's some sort of hero. What you do have to do is to separate your negative feelings for him from your desire for your children to have a good relationship with their father. Considering all the havoc the divorce is wreaking on your kids' lives, coming out of this with a good relationship with both parents would be a great consolation prize for them.

What to Do If Your Kids Don't Want to Visit Their Dad

Sometimes, particularly at first, children may be reluctant or even opposed to spending time with their dad. It can be really hard to send off your kids when they are crying or begging to stay with you. If this is the case, there are some things you can do to help them feel better about the transition:

Make sure they're not feeding off your emotions. Are you sending them the message that you miss them terribly or you're otherwise not okay without them? If so, stop. Even if you dread their being gone, this is one of those times you need to fake it until you make it. Make plans to catch up with friends or work on projects when they're gone, then let them know about your plans. (Be careful to schedule things you enjoy, but not things your kids are going to wish they could stay and do with you. Think lecture series, not World Series.) The message you want to send is that you expect them to have a nice time with their dad, and you'll be busy with your own projects and plans while they're gone. And you can all look forward to seeing each other when they get home.

Arrange for drop-off and pickup at school. Whether your kids' reluctance is due to their concern for you or not, having the exchange happen at a neutral location with only one parent there greatly reduces the chance for a meltdown. School provides the perfect opportunity. You drop them off in the morning; your ex picks them up when school gets out. The school day provides an emotional buffer between these two events that is many hours long.

Call them less. This may seem counterintuitive, but, when they are with their dad, calling them every day can make them miss you more, not less. Give them time and space to settle in at their dad's house. Calling them every two or three days is more than enough. If they're only gone for the weekend, consider not calling them at all.

Don't bulldoze their projects when they're gone. In the initial few months after we moved out, my daughter was extra sensitive about her things being exactly as she left them when she got back from weekends with her dad. If she had written on her chalkboard, for example—even if it just looked like scribbles or doodles—she would get furious if someone had added more scribbles or erased any part of them while she was away. This had less to do with any attachment to what was on the chalkboard and more to do with feeling anxious about all the changes in her life. She needed to know things would not be different when she got home.

We made a rule never to disturb her things while she was gone. If for some reason I needed to do something in her room or work on a project she had in progress, I would call her first and explain what I needed, and then have her help come up with a solution. After a few months she was back to her regular self.

Don't make your kids the go-between. If you have something you need to communicate to your ex, don't use your kids as a messenger service. Asking a kid to be your spokesperson is unfair to your child because it interferes with his relationship with his dad. Follow the guidelines for communicating with your ex covered in Chapter Four and send the message yourself.

Know when to put your kids in the driver's seat. Notwithstanding the last point, there are times when it is a good idea to put your kids in the driver's seat of communicating with their dad. Say, for example, there is a friend's birthday party that your daughter wants to attend, but the event is on a day when she is scheduled to be with her dad. Depending on your kid's age and personality, letting her take the lead on working out the schedule change with her dad can be good for everyone, but most of all for her, because it puts her in the position of having some say over her life.

On a related topic, consulting with your kid about possible changes to the custody schedule can go a long way toward making her feel empowered. I found this out the hard way with my daughter. On a couple of occasions when her dad and I needed to trade days and we worked it out without asking her first, Hannah didn't hesitate to let us know that she really didn't appreciate being left out of the dialogue. It might not always be possible to accommodate her preferences—and she understands that—but she is much more cooperative about the schedule when she's in on the conversation.

How to Handle It If Your Ex Disappoints Your Kids

If your kids are unlucky enough to have the kind of dad who disappoints them, your job is to let them vent if they need to, acknowledge their disappointment or frustration, but *still* refrain from trash-talking him. This can be tricky, so let me flesh it out with an example.

Let's say your ex promised your ten-year-old that he would come to her soccer game on Saturday and then take her out to dinner afterward. The new routine of not seeing one or the other parent for days at a stretch hasn't been easy and Emily is really looking forward to having some one-on-one time with her dad. When Saturday rolls around, her dad shows up late to the game and has his new girlfriend and her kids in tow. After the game, your ex tells Emily that they're all going to dinner together—and they're going to his new girlfriend's favorite restaurant, P. F. Chang's. Emily hates Chinese food.

When he drops Emily off at your house and you ask how dinner was, she bursts into tears. She says her dad doesn't care about her at all—he only cares about his new girlfriend. Between sobs, she adds that she hates the new girlfriend because she is a big fake and her kids are total brats.

What *not* to say. Even though you really, really want to, *don't* say something like this: "You're totally right, Emily. Your dad is such an insensitive jerk. Now you know how I felt all those years I was married to him. If he really cared about you, he wouldn't have invited them along to dinner. You should just totally blow him off from now on. And what a floozy that girlfriend is, too. I mean, where did he even meet her, anyway? Hooters?"

It might feel good to say all that, and it might even make Emily feel good in the moment, in the long run it will make her feel worse. The afterburn of hearing that her dad is a jerk is painful. The half-life of hearing her mom tell her that her dad doesn't care about her (even though Emily said it first) can last a lifetime. Saying these kinds of things to Emily can hurt her personally, damage her relationship with her dad, and corrode her relationship with you in the future. Triple points like that are anything but rewarding.

You also shouldn't say this: "Oh, Emily, you know you don't mean that. You know your dad really loves you and I'm sure his girlfriend is really nice. Once you get to know her kids, I'm sure you guys will be good friends."

That response will only upset Emily even more. She already feels like her dad caters more to his girlfriend and her kids. Now, on top of wrestling with that rejection, a response like the one above will send her the message that you don't understand how she feels at all. Or worse yet, she'll feel that you're taking his side, leaving her with zero parents in her corner.

What to say. Enough with the advice on what not to say. Here's what you *should* say:

"Ugh, Emily! That must have been *so* disappointing! You were all set for some one-on-one time with your dad, and, then, *bam*! Suddenly there are all these extra people in tow. What a bummer."

You can even add, "I get so frustrated when I'm excited about doing something with someone, and then at the last minute they either bail or change the plan without bothering to check with me."

By listening for the real feelings behind the tirade and acknowledging those, you have helped Emily to feel heard. That in turn comforts her and lessens her frustration, but it doesn't push her into deeper waters of negativity. She's upset because she was expecting and looking forward to one thing, and then the deal was switched on her at the last minute. That's what she needs to have validated. You don't need to remark one way or the other on her comments that her dad doesn't care about her, that she hates the new girlfriend, or can't stand her kids. Those statements are just the by-product of her underlying feelings of frustration and disappointment, and the underlying feelings are the only ones you need to acknowledge.

Avoid covering for their dad. Let's say your ex promised your kids that when he moved out of an apartment and bought a place of his own, the kids could get a puppy. But he ended up buying a condo downtown and decided it wasn't a good setup for a dog. Your kids are as furious as they are disappointed. Again, your job is to listen to what they have to say and acknowledge the feelings behind it. But you should *not* try to right his wrong by running out and getting them a new puppy at your house. I know it's really hard to see your kids being disappointed, but trying to fix your ex's mistakes only makes things worse. It cheats you, enables your ex, and skews your kids' expectations.

Establishing a pattern of your keeping your ex's word for him will lead to your living the life your ex promised your kids, rather than the one you choose for yourself and your family. You will find yourself taking vacations to places you never wanted to go and buying things you never wanted to own. If you make good on your ex's promises for him, you will prevent your kids from learning that keeping a promise is the specific obligation of the person who made it, and they will grow up with the mistaken impression that the world generally owes them.

In this situation, the best thing you can do for your kids is to help them learn how to handle their disappointment and adjust their expectations when dealing with someone who doesn't keep his word. These are lessons they cannot learn if you make it your mission to right all of his wrongs.

Making Seasons Bright (Even When Your Spirits Are Dim)

Observing holidays gives family life a deeper meaning and makes a house a home. But in the immediate wake of a divorce, it's hard enough to get through an average day. The pressure to conjure up fun holidays for your kids is enough to turn even the fairest of us all into a wicked witch. (If only your kid's Harry Potter costume came with some spells that *really* worked!) By modifying your holiday customs, you can create a blend of traditions that pay homage to your family's past as well as light a path to your future.

Your kids are the reason for the season. In case you're trying to figure out how you can get a hall pass on this holiday season, forget about it. Your kids need you to pull it together for them. Getting the holidays off the ground will help them understand that life goes on after divorce and send them the signal that a new sense of normal will emerge. That's a message they really need right now. And you get a present, too! By showing your kids that things will eventually be okay, you'll also be internalizing that message yourself.

▶

Be smart like the Three Wise Men. If the three kings thought one present each was good enough for the likes of the son of God, surely it's good enough for your kids, too. Set a budget for your holidays and stick to it. The idea is to maintain the practice of celebrating holidays, not to outdo your ex. Otherwise, you reduce the holidays to a popularity pageant where you and your ex compete for the kids' affections – and nothing feels more hollow than that. When the holiday season is over, you don't want your gifts to yourself to be a mountain of consumer debt and a wrecked credit score.

Rethink your holiday rituals. Sort through your family's traditions and decide which ones to keep, which to modify, and which to scrap. Say your home is the "go-to" spot in the neighborhood each Halloween because of the Camp Carnage haunted house you hold in your front yard. If you're enthusiastic about the project, you and your kids can continue this tradition. But if your ex played the pivotal part of the angry hunter who accosts the tent when everyone least expects it, you'll need to modify the tradition or scrap it in favor of doing something else. Maybe next Halloween, you could play a bitter divorced lady brandishing a stack of unpaid bills and a bottle of gin. (Kidding! Besides, that would require real acting ability since you will *never* let yourself become that character in real life. Do you hear me?)

Focus on the season, not the day. Finally, a reason to thank retailers! For decades now, they've had Christmas and other holidays on the stretching rack like a medieval torturer. Since your kids will be dividing time between two houses, the expanded holiday season gives you plenty of chances to celebrate, even if

▶

▶

you don't have the kids on the actual "day of." So, get the box of decorations out of the attic and deck out your house. Then, take advantage of all the season has to offer.

In addition to doing things at home such as carving pumpkins and baking cookies, participate in the local events scheduled for days when your kids are with you. Volunteer together at your local food bank's Thanksgiving food drive. Sign everyone up for the Jingle Bell 5K fun run. This will ensure that you and your kids come away with a horn of plenty of seasonal memories, even if you aren't together on the day itself.

Tips for flying solo. The prospect of facing your first holidays without your kids can be depressing. If you and your ex are on decent terms, you might work it out so that each parent has some time with the kids on the big day. For the rest of us mere mortals, don't sit around your empty house surrounded by reminders that you're all alone. Go to a Halloween party for grown-ups. Book a spa weekend over Thanksgiving with another single girlfriend. Spend Christmas with a relative who lives out of town.

The first holidays without your kids will pass more quickly and with fewer tears if you spend it doing something completely out of the ordinary. And don't be surprised if you come to view holidays without your kids as an opportunity to rest and recharge. Then, on the holidays you do have them, you'll be ready to make their spirits bright again.

You Still Have to Follow These Rules, Even If Your Ex Doesn't

Even if your ex is trash-talking you, blowing off his visitation, has a sitter on speed dial, or is dating up a storm, that doesn't mean you can forget about all these rules yourself. In fact, his ir-responsibility makes it even more important for you to do a good job. Ignore what your ex is up to and instead focus on doing your best to live your life right. That's the best thing for you and your kids, and the shortest road to your new normal life. Remember, you can only control how *you* handle things. So do the best you can and then relax because the rest is out of your hands.

Making an honest effort to live by these rules will go a long way toward shepherding your kids through your divorce quickly and in one piece. If you flub one or more of these rules, don't beat yourself up. Shake it off and start fresh. What we're going for here is not perfection; it's consistent effort.

The most important job you'll have in your whole life is parenting your kids. Mistakes will be made, but the goal is to have as few regrets as possible when it's all said and done. Your divorce is going to be challenging, but it will not last forever. Do your best to follow the guidelines in this chapter and you'll have plenty to be proud of.

7.

Tools to Get Over the Tool

When I was at the beginning of my divorce, I had no idea how to proceed. It wasn't just that I lacked the energy to start moving forward; I couldn't tell which way *was* forward. All I could see was murky gray or complete darkness everywhere I looked.

My mom detected my fear and paralysis with her motherly intuition. Or maybe she just clued in when she found me rocking in a fetal position in the middle of the living room floor. Either way, she recognized that I was stuck and she wanted to unstick me. So, she reached in her bag of motherly tricks and pulled out a pep talk that was two parts comfort and one part marching orders.

In the end, Mom's talk was exactly what I needed to hear. The imagery she provided helped me to focus on what I needed to do. Her frank yet encouraging tone convinced me not only that I had the power to do what needed to be done, but I had no choice but to do it. I've repeated this pep talk countless times to other women going through divorce, and I've yet to find a person who does not find it helpful. And now it's your turn to receive the eloquent wisdom that was originally gifted to me by my mother.

Taking a Different Kind of Plunge

Do you remember the childhood tale *We're Going on a Bear Hunt*? In that story, every time the storyteller encounters an obstacle—tall grass, mud, a forest, or a river—she has to figure out how to get past it. Each time the storyteller goes through the same process of elimination: You can't go over it. You can't go under it. You have to go through it.

Imagine that you are standing next to a river that is both deep and wide, and that river is filled with raw, putrid sewage. The side of the river you are standing on is completely contaminated. It is so toxic, in fact, that it can no longer support human life. The land on the other side of the river is verdant, green, and healthy. You need to permanently relocate from the contaminated side to the healthy side as soon as possible.

Just as in *We're Going on a Bear Hunt*, when it comes to crossing the river of sewage, you have no choice but to go through it. Starflight is not going to airlift you from one side to the other. There are no boats or rubber rafts to ride on. There's neither time nor materials to build a bridge. You don't even get any arm floaties. The only way for you to get from one side to the other is to swim.

In light of that fact, your job is to find the shortest route across that river, jump in, and go as fast as you can. Be sure to swim in a straight line. Don't meander off course or stop to tread water because that will only make the crossing take longer. And once you're in, there's no turning back. The side you came from is contaminated, and if you go back you'll only have to start all over again. The only thing worse than swimming across the river of sewage is swimming partway across, going back, and then having to swim across a second time. While you're swimming, make sure you don't get any of the sewage in your mouth. That stuff is poison. Even soaking in it is bad for you, so your goal is to get out of it as fast as you can.

The river of sewage analogy can serve as a valuable tool in helping you size up issues that arise during your divorce. Do you want to dig in on something? Ask yourself whether doing so is consistent with taking the most direct route across the river. Will fighting for it get you to the other side or make you stop and tread water for a while? Will it move you backward or even force you to swallow a big mouthful of sewage? Thinking of it in that context will help lead you to the right answer.

So, now you know what you're up against. It's not going to be fun, and the sooner you get it over with, the better. But before you jump in, I have a surprise for you. You don't get any arm floaties, but you do get a toolkit stocked with all kinds of gadgets that will come in very handy along the way.

Get Kitted Up

Just as it takes a village to raise a child, it takes a toolkit to divorce a tool. Below is a list of all the tools in your kit and instructions on how to use each one for the maximum benefit. There is room in your kit for additional gadgets, devices, and strategies you will pick up along the way, whether you find them in future chapters of this book, get them from other people, or craft them yourself. By the end of this chapter, you will be well equipped to take the plunge into the river of sewage and start swimming like crazy for the other side.

Recruit your A-Team. I pity the fool who tries to go through a divorce without a personal A-Team. Your A-Team consists of two or three friends you can count on through thick and thin, like maybe your sister and your two very best friends. Before you appoint anyone, make sure you give it some thought. What's your history with each person? Has your relationship always been strong and steady or are you on-again-off-again friends? Is she not only good at listening but also good at keeping confidences?

These are the people you will turn to whenever you need a shoulder to cry on or someone to vent to. Sometimes you may need them to shake you and tell you to snap out of it, and other times they may need to help pick up the pieces when you fall apart. Make sure the friends you put on your A-Team are rock solid and have the requisite skills to do the job.

Once you've decided who qualifies, offer them a spot on the team and explain what it involves. It's important that you ask them, rather than simply assuming they're cool with it. They need to know you are counting on them—and you need to know that you can.

To get the maximum benefit out of your A-Team, you have to use it correctly. Go to members of your A-Team when you need to spill your guts, and limit how much you blab about your divorce to everyone else. This way you'll control how much of your personal business gets out on the street.

Don't deplete your resources. Yes, you are going through something really huge and terrible right now, but it's important for you to remember that other people have lives, too. Leaning on your A-Team is fine—after all, that's what it's there for. But you also need to ask your friends how things are going with them, too. And then, you have to be quiet and listen while they answer. This may not be as easy as it sounds.

At a time when you're learning the details about your ex's secret other family, it can be hard to muster genuine support for your friend whose biggest problem is keeping secret the surprise birthday party she's planning for her amazing husband. But it is important that you at least act as if you care. Sure, your problems are objectively bigger than hers right now. That's not the point, though. It's a friendship, not a crisis competition. And friendship is a two-way street.

A good way to build some balance into your relationship with your friend/sister/neighbor is to make a habit of letting her go first. Ask her what's going on with her job, family, or kids, and give her the floor. Only after she's had a chance to tell you what's on her mind—and you've listened and even asked follow-up questions—do you launch into the latest chapter of your troubles. Right now, there are not enough hours in the day to fully exhaust the topic of how badly your life sucks. By letting your friends go first, you will safeguard against spending the entirety of every conversation talking only about yourself.

Otherwise, you run the risk of burning out the members of your A-team precisely when you need them the most. Even the

Tools to Get Over the Tool • 113

most giving friend can experience compassion fatigue if she constantly listens to you talk about your problems but never gets any support in return. After a while that friend will stop taking your calls.

Not only do your friends need a break from hearing about your downer of a divorce, you need one, too—whether or not you realize it. Any time you spend sympathizing or strategizing about the problems or issues in their lives, you are not obsessing over your own. This is a critical part of retraining your brain and making space, time, and energy for a new normal life—a key to staying out of the divortex.

Rock your Girl Power Playlist. Music can have a powerful effect on your mood. A song that resonates with you can take you from melancholy to marvelous—or vice versa—in under a stanza. A carefully constructed Girl Power Playlist can overhaul your mood when your divorce gets you down, but not any breakup song will do. As entertaining as old school hits like Tammy Wynette's "D-I-V-O-R-C-E" may be, breakup songs that focus on sadness or regret have no place on your Girl Power Playlist. Songs have to strike the right tone both musically and lyrically to make the cut.

These days, there are plenty of songs to choose from, and no one deserves more credit for that than Alanis Morissette. In 1995, Morissette ushered in a new era for breakup songs with her eyebrow-singeing anthem "You Oughta Know." This was not your mother's breakup song. Morissette sounds like she's one Red Bull away from throwing a chainsaw in the trunk of her car and heading to her ex's house. But as entertaining as it may be, this song does not belong on your Girl Power Playlist because it's loaded with misdirected anger. Rather than using her anger the way Adele does—as fuel to move her past her breakup—Morissette squanders it by using it to blowtorch her ex.

To qualify for your Girl Power Playlist, a song must meet the following criteria:

- **Its style must resonate with you.** For a breakup song to be effective, you have to actually want to listen to it. You won't find any kick-ass Miranda Lambert breakup songs on my Girl Power Playlist—not because they don't exist, but because I can't stand country and western music. And a badass folk breakup song (should one ever be written) could never be on my Girl Power Playlist because folk music puts me in a coma, and it's hard to feel empowered when you're unconscious. The best place to find Girl Power songs for your playlist is on a radio station that plays the kind of music you enjoy.

- **It must have a message of post-breakup empowerment.** It's fine for the song to acknowledge either how much the relationship sucked or how painful the breakup was, but the upshot has to be that the singer is moving on and is stronger, happier, or better off. In other words, some treatment of the past is okay, but the main focus of the song must be on the future. A perfect example of this is Katy Perry's song "Roar."

- **It cannot express a longing to get back together.** Remember, a Girl Power Playlist is supposed to move you forward, not push you backward. Any song that indicates that the singer is lost rather than better off without him is counterproductive. So, Matchbox 20's "If You're Gone" or Bruno Mars's "When I Was Your Man" are both definite nos.

- **It cannot focus on catching a new man.** Any song about getting a new guy is automatically disqualified—this rule eliminates a lot of songs. In this type of song, the singer usually wants to get a new man to prove to her ex that he made a big mistake. In other words, she is focusing on her ex, his reactions, and his feelings, rather than focusing on herself or her new love interest. This means she's squandering her resources on her ex rather than using them for herself or her new relationship. In the song "Irreplaceable," Beyoncé tells her cheating ex that she "can have another 'you' in a minute." Why would she want another "him"? Loser guys are a dime a dozen, so replacing one with another isn't anything to crow about. As much as I love Beyoncé, "Irreplaceable" doesn't make the cut.

Three of my favorite breakup songs are "Stronger" by Kelly Clarkson, "So What" by P!nk, and "Wide Awake" by Katy Perry. If you like pop music, that trio of songs (or others by those same artists) would make an excellent start for your Girl Power Playlist. Although the lyrics of these songs are not 100 percent Emotional Hardbody–approved, they are about as close to perfect as I have found. Plus, the overall vibe of each song is fantastic—empowered and focused on the future, using anger as fuel to move on.

If you want to rock it old school and pay homage to the women who went before us, consider including "I Will Survive" by Gloria Gaynor, "These Boots Are Made for Walking" by Nancy Sinatra, and "Respect" by Aretha Franklin on your playlist. Load these songs on your smartphone and add your own favorites as you go along. Then, whenever your divorce has you down, cue up your Girl Power Playlist for an instant attitude adjustment.

Make support symbols your new eye candy. Forget sex symbols. When it comes to getting through your divorce, there's nothing better to feast your eyes on than support symbols. A support symbol is any object that makes you feel strong, hopeful, happy, lucky, comforted, loved, or all of the above. Remember in the *Peanuts* comic strip how Linus would turn to his trusty blanket when he needed to get centered? His blanket was his support symbol. Whether it's a lucky penny you found in the parking lot when you left your lawyer's office the day you hired her, or that winning scratch-off ticket you bought at the gas station the day your ex moved out, if it makes you feel good, it counts as a support symbol.

I had several support symbols that I leaned on heavily during my divorce. One was a heart-shaped sticky note that read "Have a nice day!" that my sister Angela stuck on a magazine article she mailed to me a week or two after I moved into my new house. From the moment I saw that sticky note, I knew it was turbocharged with soothing powers. It reminded me of my sister, and thinking about her made me feel reassured and supported. I taped that sticky note to the edge of my computer screen. Whenever I got an email about my divorce and my stomach would start to knot up, I would glance at that sticky note and feel better instantly.

Another one of my favorite support symbols was a label my daughter made me that read "BEST MOMMY EVER." I stuck it to my bathroom mirror, and every time I brushed my teeth I was reminded of how much my daughter loved me.

Keep your eyes peeled for random objects that mean something to you. Then place these support symbols in strategic locations, such as on your nightstand, in your gym bag, on your keychain, on your desk, or in your car. That way, you will always be within range of the support that these symbols radiate.

Canonize a divorce patron saint. There will be times during your divorce when you feel that you just don't have it in you to keep fighting your way toward the finish line. These are the times when your divorce patron saint can carry you forward, just as Jesus did in that corny "Footprints in the Sand" poem. A divorce patron saint is someone whom you love dearly and who is or has been vitally important to you in your life. Your divorce patron saint can be living or dead. Maybe it's your grandmother, who was always there for you and would never want to see you give up on yourself. Maybe it's a teacher who really believed in you. When you feel you can't be strong for you, think about your divorce patron saint and draw strength from her.

Choose your divorce role model. This period in your life is daunting. Your regular life is gone and you don't yet know what your future will look like. That uncertainty can be scary. Having a divorce role model can help reassure you that you're going to be okay.

Designate someone you know who has already gone through a divorce—someone who lived through the hell you're living through right now and has since rebuilt her life. Pick someone who is happy and whose kids seem to have adjusted well. Whether or not you tell her is up to you, but there's no reason you have to. If you'd rather choose someone you don't know personally, that's fine, too. But make sure you pick someone who conducted herself responsibly during her divorce and now lives a healthy life. When it comes to celebrity examples, Katie Holmes passes the test, but Britney Spears does not.

Take breakup breaks. It's never too soon to start practicing how *not* to think about your divorce. Like a baby bird learning to fly, you won't nail it on the first try. That's where breakup breaks come in handy. Designate an activity you can do with a friend that will take a defined length of time—not too long, but not too short. Say, going for coffee or a short walk. Tell your friend that you would like to try to use the opportunity to take a break from thinking or talking about your divorce. Then (and this is the hard part) stick to it, even if your friend brings it up.

Going to a movie is a good activity to start with because (unless you're like my mom) you don't talk in a movie theater. This exercise might strike you as either too gimmicky or simple to be useful, but, before you pass judgment, try it out. You'll be surprised at how hard it is to pull off—and how worthwhile it is if you do. In fact, it's so challenging that you should designate a code word to use—such as "boring"—in case one of you accidentally brings up your divorce.

Then, you can discuss subjects you don't normally get a chance to talk about because you're too busy bringing people up to speed on your divorce drama. This exercise is excellent training for moving on—and it also gives you a meaningful rest from obsessing over all the details of your divorce.

Picture imperfect. A picture is worth a thousand hours of therapy—isn't that how the saying goes? The truth is, everyone takes a bad picture once in a while, and that's not necessarily a bad thing. Find a really bad photo of your ex and keep it handy. It doesn't have to be a photo that looks objectively ridiculous. It could be one in which you see something subtle that reminds you of one of your ex's numerous character flaws, like his impatience, arrogance, or insecurity.

Maybe it's a photo of him on Christmas Eve at your parents'

house and he's doing that fake smile thing he always did when your mom was talking to him. Or maybe it's a photo from your birthday party and he's checking his watch while everyone else is singing "Happy Birthday" to you. Whenever you start to feel nostalgic about your marriage, take a glance at that photo and you'll remember exactly why you are getting a divorce.

You can do this without photos, too. The trick is to think of one of his grating characteristics (like his "cool guy" voice), favorite fashion statements (that puffy vest with high-waisted jeans), or ridiculous catchphrases ("Get 'er done!"). Cue up the mental audio or video of one of these gems and your resolve will get an instant power boost.

Make a list like Santa. One of the reasons divorce is so hard is that it involves losing the love and support of the one person you, at least at one point in time, thought you would be able to count on until the day you died. If the divorce is prompted by the discovery of a betrayal such as an affair, that makes it even harder. It's not uncommon for people to feel abandoned and totally alone in these initial days.

To remind yourself of all the people in your life who are there for you, learn a lesson from Santa and create your own "nice" list. Write down everyone you can think of—friends and family—whose friendship you can count on right now. Watching the list grow as you write down name after name is incredibly therapeutic. It makes you realize and appreciate how much support you actually have, and that engenders feelings of empowerment.

8.

Search and Rescue

(Rediscovering Your Personal Identity)

I have an assignment for you, should you choose to accept it: It's a search-and-rescue mission. Here's the profile of the person you're looking for: a normally together woman who is temporarily, but totally, knocked off her game by her divorce. That's right. You're looking for yourself. But I don't mean the person you were right before the divorce bomb went off; I mean the essence of you. You may not have seen her in quite some time, so you're going to need to think long and hard before you can develop a composite sketch.

Here's the thing about your wedding dress that no one told you: It shrinks—and I'm not talking about the fabric. The dress shrinks what's inside it: namely, you. Traditional lore holds that we are all supposed to grow up and find the man of our dreams, get married, and magically become "one" with him. If you were to sketch out on a cocktail napkin a healthy version of what that looks like, it would involve a Venn diagram in which you and your husband are each represented by a separate circle, but you overlap some, too.

That sort of configuration is all well and good, since it involves each of you maintaining your own individual identities. But all too often, women get completely consumed by their marriages to the point where there is no part of their own identity left. There's just one circle on the cocktail napkin and you're lost somewhere in it, but it's not at all clear where.

When I Filed My Missing Person Report

People tend to remember exactly where they were when they got some bad news, such as when the president was assassinated or the space shuttle blew up. I'll never forget where I was when I realized my marriage had completely obliterated my identity. It was at Whole Foods Market.

Until the day I gave birth to my daughter, I had what was the perfect law job for me. I worked as an attorney, but I had only one client—a telecommunications company. The job was interesting enough and I got to work at home. For me, this combination proved to be the best of all worlds. I worked long hours at something I enjoyed and I was able to keep up with things at home at the same time.

Right around the time Hannah was born the work dried up. The timing was perfect. Fortunately, our financial situation enabled us to live more than comfortably on one income, and the fact that the work simply vanished meant I didn't have to choose between a rewarding but demanding job and being with Hannah. The choice was made for me.

Five years later, a lawyer friend called me with an opportunity: Whole Foods Market was looking for its first in-house real estate lawyer. My friend knew one of the decision makers, and she thought my previous work experience, as well as my personal profile as an exercise-loving vegetarian and native Austinite, made me a natural fit for the position. Although I wasn't considering going back to work at the time, there were two fears in the back of my head that convinced me to see where the discussions led.

First, I had a sense that I might not be able to count on That Man or my marriage. I was no longer working, which meant I had no independent source of income. That Man was not forthcoming, so I knew very little about the details of our finances. I signed on none of his bank accounts, yet he signed on all of mine. Sometime during that same year, I found out that, without mentioning it to me first, he had gone to lunch with the lawyer who had drafted our wills to ask him about rewriting them to change what my son would receive in the event of our death—and not for the better. Given my husband's controlling nature and secretive ways, I was beginning to think that I could, at any moment, find myself in a position where I needed to support myself.

Second, as a lawyer who had been out of the workforce for more than five years, I was worried that this might be the very last time someone thought of me when a job opportunity arose. Never having met a dollar he didn't like, That Man clearly wanted me to pursue this job—not enough to agree to take on a meaningful amount of workload at home should I end up going back to work, but enough to enthusiastically encourage me to chase down the lead. Over the years I had been staying home with Hannah, I had gotten the sense that he felt my law degree was an unused asset in his portfolio that he desperately wanted to put to work, and the only thing standing in the way was me.

I think he had expected that I would not be content for long and would want to return to work. That way, he would have gotten the benefit of the increased household income while also getting the credit for both "allowing" me to stay at home with Hannah for as long as I wanted, and then being supportive of me when I elected to return to work. The fact that I really and truly enjoyed being a stay-at-home mom was thwarting his plans.

I went through multiple interviews with various decision makers at Whole Foods over several weeks. During the entire process, I wrestled with not wanting to leave Hannah and take on a demanding full-time job. I was upfront about how I had not been looking for a job and how much I enjoyed staying home with my daughter. And even though I didn't know the details of our finances, this much was clear: That Man and I didn't need the money to make ends meet. (But that didn't seem to make That Man want that money any less.) When the discussions resulted in an offer, I negotiated a deal that allowed me to pick up my daughter from school and then work from home for the remaining few hours of each day.

The salary was substantially less than what I had been making five years earlier when I'd exited the workforce, so taking this job was going to make my life much more complicated in exchange for a relatively modest amount of money. And out of my modest pay, I'd have to hire a sitter for Hannah while I cranked out the last few hours of work each day. This meant I'd be paying someone to hang out with Hannah while I prepared real estate documents, when the truth was I would much prefer to be hanging out with Hannah to begin with. No amount of negotiation skills could make that a good deal for me. But once they had agreed to my flexibility requests and had come up (even if only modestly) on salary, I felt obligated to take the job.

Everyone at Whole Foods was very friendly. That morning on my very first day, people stopped by my windowless office to introduce themselves. But by early afternoon I noticed something strange. As soon as it was my turn to talk, the only words that came out of my mouth were about That Man. Some people talked about their significant others, too, but the key difference was they had plenty of other topics in their repertoire. From outside interests to work issues to funny personal stories, these people were adept at the art of spinning the conversational lazy Susan.

For me, though, the wheel always landed on the topic of That Man. They would talk about volunteer work. I would tell them about my husband's favorite cause. They would tell a story about a mix-up involving their wedding invitations. I would tell them my husband owned a commercial printing company. They would talk about their plan to spend Christmas in New Mexico. I would tell them my husband used to live in Santa Fe.

It didn't take me (or anyone else) long to notice this tic of mine. You know how some people constantly pepper their speech with fillers like "um" or "like"? My speech was constantly peppered with references to That Man. But noticing it and stopping it were two different matters. I immediately resolved to make a conscious effort to talk about other things instead. But try as I might, I couldn't string together a sentence that didn't include him.

That's when it all clicked for me. Over the course of the five years that I had been staying at home, my identity had gotten smaller and smaller until it finally reached a point at which I had no independent identity left. And the spooky thing was, I hadn't even noticed it happening. I could talk about That Man. I could talk about my kids. But unless we were talking about me from more than five years ago, I had nothing to say. The reason was as simple as it was sad: There was no independent me left.

I don't blame my disappearance on the institution of marriage or being a stay-at-home mom. Plenty of women get married or stay home with their kids and maintain their own identities. I don't even blame it on That Man. So why did my individual identity disappear? I believe it was a combination of two factors. First, I was raised with the conventional dogma that when two people get married, they become one. Since my divorce, I've come to believe that, even as a metaphor, this message is risky for women. But when I first married my husband I had not figured that out yet. Back then, I desperately wanted this marriage to work, so I threw myself into it and tried to do everything right. I'm not saying I was perfect—far from it—but I was definitely all in.

Now I know that was a mistake. Being enthusiastic is fine, but I should have maintained my identity and independence. Maintaining your independence doesn't mean hedging your bets in case the marriage fails; it means leaving enough room to be healthy. And you can't have a healthy marriage without healthy individuals.

Which brings me to the second factor. Once it was clear to me that my marriage was damaged, I kept pouring more time and energy into the sinking ship. Rather than strapping on some life jackets, pumping up the emergency raft, and preparing to transport family members from one craft to the other should the need arise, I kept clinging to the damaged vessel. A wiser, healthier, more independent person would have recognized the danger and come up with a evacuation plan. But I was so consumed with trying to keep my marriage from going under that I didn't even realize I was drowning and my kids were in danger.

It wasn't until I was in an environment where I was expected to function as an individual that I noticed I was MIA. I suddenly realized I had a ton of work to do, but it wasn't for Whole Foods. I needed to figure out who and where I was. So, after three days in a position that many lawyers would have killed for, I walked into my boss's office and gave my best George Costanza "It's not you, it's me" impersonation—which, conveniently, was the God's honest truth.

I concluded that if I really believed there was a significant risk that my marriage could implode (and I did), it was likely that I would end up reentering the workforce at that time. That meant the first order of business was for me to locate my personal identity, because the first step to performing well at any job was to show up. My three days at Whole Foods had made clear that, as long as my personal identity was MIA, I couldn't do that.

Be Your Own Best Friend

The exhilarating thing about reconnecting with the real you is that it feels like being reunited with a long-lost friend, and it couldn't come at a better time. But you have to find your identity first before you can celebrate your reunion with it. After I discovered that my identity was AWOL, it took me another two years to locate it. I knew my identity wasn't in the house I "shared" with That Man. From the issues of *Cowboys and Indians* magazine stacked on end tables to the furniture that was as grand as it was faux, I came to see that house as an embarrassing attempt to convey an image that he so desperately wished was his own—something akin to a wealthy cattle baron from a prominent family in the southwestern United States, rather than an average-yet-persnickety Joe from Iowa. And because "our" house was packed to the rafters with half a century of his attempts to overcompensate for his perceived shortcomings, there wasn't room for my personality, let alone my hopes and dreams.

The first morning in my new house, I finally reconnected with the real me. When I opened my eyes that morning, I realized that, notwithstanding the fear and sadness I was struggling with, I had been smiling in my sleep. I knew that, despite the difficult road ahead, I had done something that had taken a massive pair of ovaries: I had taken a giant first step to getting back to being me.

I got out of bed and walked downstairs to make a pot of coffee. At my new house there was only one coffeepot on the kitchen counter—my coffeepot—rather than the two that had sat on our kitchen counter in the old house. I liked my coffee strong, but it was not strong enough for a pretend cattle baron's palate, forged from years of make-believe campfire breakfasts on the imaginary sprawling family ranch. He insisted upon two separate pots. It seems even when it came to coffee, That Man and I could not find common ground.

I lit a scented candle, something I used to love before I got married but had to stop when scented candles landed on the long and ever-changing list of things to which he was "allergic." I turned on the radio and *Car Talk* was on, a show that my son and I used to love but that I had not listened to in years because That Man thought it was annoying. I looked around at all the boxes that I needed to unpack and, although it was daunting, I was excited about setting things up the way I wanted to. For the first time in years, I felt like I had found myself again. I had opinions, tastes, and preferences that mattered. I was finally home.

The search that had begun at Whole Foods a couple of years earlier was over. But although I was home, that didn't mean it was time to relax. Tons of work was ahead of me.

Fire Your Flare Gun

If you have not begun your own reconnaissance mission, it's time for you to get started. The first step in the process requires you to think. A lot. About yourself. I know that sounds strange. After all, too much time spent navel-gazing is rarely a good thing. But right now, it's just what the doctor ordered.

Take a look inside yourself and see if you can find your long-lost personality—the one that got buried underneath your husband's identity and your role as wife and mother. Then put that identity front and center. Don't worry. Your role as mother isn't going anywhere. It will still be as important as it always was, perhaps even more important, considering what your kids are going through. But your individual identity will be making a big comeback.

Fill in the blanks. You know those *American Girl* activity books that have page after page of fill-in-the-blank questions for girls and their best friends to answer to determine how well they know each other? For the next several weeks, I want you to act as if you are answering all those questions about yourself. Don't get hung up on huge questions, such as "What do I want to do with the rest of my life?" Those can be overwhelming. Instead, start with the basics.

Make it a point to be more aware of your own thoughts and opinions in any given situation. While you go about your everyday life, pay attention to your likes and dislikes. What sparks your interest? What puts you off? Take note of your preferences on matters big and small. From songs on the radio and cars on the road to political movements and philosophies, keep a running list of things you love and things you hate—ideas you support and those you oppose. You can even get your kids involved in this exercise; they'd probably welcome a chance to focus on something not related to the divorce. Getting in touch with these ideas is all part of clarifying who you are.

From there, you can move onto bigger questions, including:

- As a young adult, what did you want to do with your life?

- How did you spend your free time before you were married? What were your hobbies or interests? Do any of those still interest you today? If not, can you think of any topics related to those interests that you find compelling?

- What are (or were) your pipe dreams? What would you do if you didn't have anything tying you down? Acknowledging these dreams can help you become aware of what makes you tick. It can also help you figure out new projects that incorporate those interests. Have you fantasized about going on

safari? Maybe a film series on Africa would satisfy your wanderlust. Have you nibbled on the idea of opening a restaurant?
Perhaps taking a cooking class would sate that hunger.

- What were your favorite classes in college? Are there books,
  movies, or excursions that can help you pick up where you left
  off? Did you love taking Spanish? See if there's an informal
  conversation group you can join. Was art history your favorite? Get exhibition schedules for the museums in your area,
  and take day and weekend trips to check them out.

Here are a few additional actions to take:

- Go to the bookstore and wander through the rows of books
  and magazines. Find three magazines and three books that
  interest you, and then give some thought to why they caught
  your eye.

- Keep a pad and pen handy—in your purse, in the car, on the
  kitchen counter, at your desk. When you are listening to the
  radio, watching the news, or just having lunch, write down
  any topic that pops into your head that you would like to
  know more about. Then follow through on checking it out.

- Look over the course schedule for the nearest community college. See if there are any classes that strike your fancy.

- Check bulletin boards at coffee shops or local universities as
  well as online resources such as Meetup.com for get-togethers
  on topics that interest you. Lectures and meetings will provide

you with the chance to learn more about something you enjoy, as well as meet people who share your interests.

Collect more clues. As you begin to sleuth out the whereabouts of the various pieces of your identity and put them back together, it helps to have physical clues. Round up tokens that represent different facets of your personality—things that remind you of exactly who you are. While I was engaged in the process of reclaiming my identity, I collected and displayed souvenirs that reminded me of where I had come from, including photographs of ancestors who had died before I was born, and a map of Italy, the birthplace of my grandparents. I also collected and displayed reminders of facets of my identity that were forged more recently, such as my "Colgate Mom" coffee mug from when my son was in college. I liked being surrounded by items that reflected who I was and how I fit into the world around me. Whether it's a necklace your parents gave you when you were little or a cookbook that belonged to your grandmother, these items can sharpen the lines around how you define yourself.

Learn Italian. Wives and mothers tend to prioritize everyone else's needs over their own. We don't just feel it is part of the job description of these two roles; we were enculturated to believe it is at the very heart of being a woman. Girls are raised to be good wives and mothers, which translates to being endlessly giving and nurturing. This leads most women to adopt an "after you" policy: We spend our entire lives making sure everyone else is taken care of and letting everyone else go first.

There's nothing wrong with this if you're in the company of people who are similarly considerate. In that context, the "after you" policy results in people taking turns, with adjustments factored in for varying levels of age and ability, which works out well for everyone. But if you are in the company of someone who always goes first, and never recognizes that it is your (or anyone else's) turn, not only is that not fair to you, it's actually not good for him.

My sister Monica teaches Italian and has spent a lot of time in Italy. I first visited that country when I tagged along with her on a trip with some of her high school students. Before we landed, she explained some local customs so we would not accidentally run afoul of them. One of these customs had to do with taking turns. In bakeries, coffee shops, ticket counters, or stores, American tourists of the nonugly variety have a tendency to wait for the person in charge to signal that it is his or her turn to order or check out.

Rather than viewing this as being polite, Italians are likely to view it as being inconsiderate. Your failure to pay attention to when it's your turn puts pressure on everyone else, including the shopkeeper, and it gums up the system. You feel slighted because other people keep cutting in front of you while you're being patient and polite. Other customers get irritated at you because your lack of attention and assertiveness slows down the line. The shopkeeper gets annoyed because he has enough to do without keeping track of when it's your turn and inviting you to take it. Monica instructed us that it was our job to notice when it was our turn, to be ready when it was, and then to promptly and unapologetically take it.

After we landed in Rome and collected our luggage, we popped into a busy convenience store in the airport to buy some bottles of water. I had my wallet out and was ready to pay, but I did not step up fast enough when the person in front of me concluded his purchase. While I waited for the cashier to signal that it was my turn to approach, another customer swooped in front of me and plopped his gum and candy bar on the counter. The cashier got annoyed, but not with the customer who swooped in. He was annoyed with me for not doing my part to keep things orderly, efficient, and fair.

Without the benefit of Monica's explanation, the cashier's behavior would have struck us all as rude, and we would have formed a negative impression of Italians before we even left the airport. But Monica's coaching caused us to see the episode in another light entirely. We weren't helpless and so we shouldn't act as if it were up to other people to prod us along or tend to our needs. In every setting, we were members of a larger group and we each had a responsibility to do our part to move things along.

The lesson that Monica taught me was one of the many reasons why that trip to Italy was life-changing. I realized that for my entire marriage I had been waiting for my turn to come on matters big and small. From what restaurants we ate at, to where we spent our vacations, to how the house was furnished, to what I cooked for dinner, I generally put what I wanted last. At first, I did it because I wanted to be a "good" wife and mother, and I thought my turn would eventually come. But after years of getting passed over, I realized the precedent had been established that I never got a turn, and I resented it. The trip to Italy made me realize that it was not fair to expect anyone else but me to see to it that I got my turn. I could hardly fault my husband for not ever allowing me to have a turn if I never asked for it.

When it comes to your turn, it's up to you to take it. It's your turn.

9.

The Divortex
(the Gravitational Force That Keeps You Orbiting Your Past)

You've heard of black holes in outer space, right? Wikipedia describes them as regions of "space-time" (I'm not even going to pretend I understand what that is, although it sounds like a really fun place for a kid to have an astronaut-themed birthday party) surrounded by a surface called the "event horizon." Once anything, including light, hits the event horizon, it has reached a point of no return. It gets sucked into the black hole and gravity prevents it from escaping.

The divortex presents a similar risk. Its gravitational force captures people who are going through divorce, forcing all their thoughts and energy to orbit their now-ending marriages and their soon-to-be exes. Much like a black hole, the divortex will suck all the light out of your life. By sentencing all your thoughts to constantly revolve around your defunct marriage, the divortex keeps you trapped in your past, robs you of your present, and creates a roadblock to your future. Your goal is not to get pulled in. And if you do find yourself trapped there, your job is to do whatever it takes to break out of it.

Once you get past the initial phase of your divorce—the one in which your sole objective was to hold it together enough to get through each day—things shift gears a bit. A new daily rhythm emerges, and the energy you had to dedicate to simply putting one foot in front of the other becomes available to focus on something else. That's exactly when you are at the greatest risk of getting sucked into the divortex. Think of it this way: When you till a plot of land, if you don't fill the space with plants you want, other plants will crop up instead. Don't let the bitter weeds and thorny vines of your past take root. Fill your life with something that will bear healthy fruit.

Conventional conditioning makes women easy prey for the divortex. From the time they are little, girls dream about growing up and getting married. Then, as newlyweds, women tend to think first and foremost about their marriages. When things begin to deteriorate, they double-down and put even more effort and energy into their relationship. This consistent effort makes constantly thinking about their marriage second nature. When it becomes clear that divorce is inevitable, constantly thinking about their marriage morphs into constantly thinking about their divorce. This happens automatically—like breathing. Only unlike breathing, obsessing over your ex is not good for your health.

Breaking out of this obsessive focus on the past requires actively directing your attention to your present or what's ahead. While the process of rediscovering who you are now can be helpful in this effort, the initial period can stir up a range of emotions—and not all of them are positive. The realization that your own tastes, preferences, opinions, and ideas actually matter again can make you euphoric. That's exactly how I felt that first morning in my new house. But this rediscovery may underscore how long it's been since they mattered to anyone and that can cause you to start stewing over the past again. Euphoria is an emotion that places you in the present and points you to the future, while regret mires you in the past.

This battle between your past and your future is at the very heart of the work that is ahead of you. The longer it takes for you to break free from the divortex, the longer it will take for you to size up the roads that presently lie before you, and you will have less time to spend traveling down them. Do not waste the burst of energy that accompanies rediscovering who you are by wallowing in regret over the years you spent allowing your opinions to be discounted, your preferences to be ignored, and your personality to be marginalized.

Do as Eminem Says, Not as He Does

Eminem had a song in 2002 called "Cleanin' Out My Closet" in which he overshares about his dysfunctional relationship with his mom, and catalogs all of the ways she went wrong when raising him. Judging from the lyrics and his delivery, it sounds as if he isn't cleaning out his closet as much as he is simply conducting a public inventory of the entire mess he keeps crammed inside it.

Even if Eminem can't follow his own advice, you can. When it comes to things that remind you of your ex or your marriage, either get them out of the house altogether or at least put them away so that you won't have to come across them all the time. Round up, box up, and put in storage any gifts he gave you (assuming he ever did that sort of thing), any mementos having to do with vacations you took together, or reminders of your wedding (your ring, your dress, your photos).

Then, notify your lawyer in your weekly roundup email that you have these items boxed up and stored. Don't dispose of these items without clearing it with your lawyer first, even if you think they are rightfully yours. There may be temporary orders in place that prevent you from taking any action like that right now, and you don't want to run afoul of them.

When it comes to items that either belong to him or you know are significant to him—like his Big Mouth Billy Bass that hangs in his man cave or the autographed photo of Chuck Norris he kept tacked on the wall in the garage—don't succumb to the temptation to deliver these items to your ex yourself. Even if you are as selfless as Mother Teresa and have no ulterior motive, these deliveries almost always lead to conflict. If you really want your divorce to go smoothly, it's simply not worth the risk.

Here's another bad idea: driving to his house without calling first and dumping his stuff on his front lawn. That can (and will) backfire in no fewer than a dozen different ways. Also in the "bad idea" department: tossing his stuff in the nearest dumpster or running his items through your paper shredder. As good as that might feel in the moment, it will not be worth the blowback when your ex and his lawyer cite it as convincing evidence of how spiteful and crazy you are.

Although these items may be a source of irritation to you, they may well have value in your divorce process in that they can be used as leverage when it comes to getting him to accommodate your requests. So box up his things and put them somewhere safe, until you can work out a plan through your respective lawyers to get the items back to him. The name of the game here is to get all the items that remind you of your marriage or your ex out of your line of sight in your everyday life so they do not serve as a one-way ticket into the divortex.

Keep Busy

As fantastic as it is to be in an environment that has enough oxygen for your real personality to return, you may also have an abundance of something else that may not be quite as fantastic for you right now: time all by your lonesome. Sometimes spending time by yourself can be a welcome novelty, but other times being home alone when your kids are with their dad can leave you vulnerable to getting sucked into orbiting your past.

During the first six months in my new house, I could not stand to spend evenings at home alone when Hannah was at her dad's house. Being alone during the day was okay, and at night while I was sleeping was also manageable. But for some reason, spending an evening at home alone was completely depressing for me. Staying in the house would trigger a downward spiral and I'd end up pacing the floors all night. In the morning, I was too weak to resist getting pulled back into the divortex.

The best way to prevent this is to anticipate these blocks of time and fill them with constructive activities that will keep you busy and entertained.

- **Take the initiative.** Don't sit around and wait for friends to call you with invitations. You know when your kids will be with their dad, so be proactive. Call or email your friends and make plans to have dinner or see a movie.

- **Never say never.** I promise this is the closest I'll ever get to recommending that you listen to Justin Bieber. But during this initial phase of your divorce, you would do well to adopt a policy of accepting all invitations that don't have "irresponsible," "trouble," or "crazy" written on them. The benefits of this policy are numerous. First, accepting invitations leads to getting more invitations. (And the opposite is also true, by the way: The more invitations you decline, the fewer you will receive.) You want all the invitations you can get right now, provided they are to events, activities, or get-togethers that don't reflect poorly on you. (Think book club, not strip club.) So, say yes to as many as reasonably possible.

  Even when it comes to things that you normally wouldn't be interested in, adopt a "fifteen minutes" policy and stop by just long enough to say hi and give the event a chance. Now is a perfect time to try new things. Even if you've never fancied yourself as a future Kendra Scott, fifteen minutes at your co-worker's jewelry-making party will be fifteen fewer minutes at home alone, and you may meet new people or discover new activities that you enjoy.

- **Be resourceful.** Know where to look to get information on events in your town. Whether it's the daily newspaper, an alternative arts and culture publication, a digital magazine, or a public radio station website, pick the outlets that best match your interests and personality, and monitor them for activities that sound interesting to you.

- **Have a backup plan.** No matter how well you plan, you will sometimes find yourself with a block of time and nothing to do. For these occasions, have a couple of places mapped out where you can safely fly solo. Sometimes I still find the prospect of spending the evening home alone working on my laptop to be super depressing. But spending a few hours with my laptop at a neighborhood coffee shop is not just fine, it's entertaining. Bookstores, gyms, and movie theaters are also great backup plans. It's a good idea to have more than one place scoped out so you can have different options depending on what kind of mood you're in.

Don't Overshare About Your Ex.

You may not know it yet, but you have a ton going for you right now. You've launched a search and rescue mission for your personal identity. You've committed to keeping track of and taking your turn when it rolls around. You are at the very beginning of a new era in your personal life—an era that promises new friendships and adventures. Don't dim your chance to establish a bright new future by steering all conversation toward your divorce. I'm not asking you to conceal the fact that you're getting one or to pretend you've never been married. But I am begging you to refrain from blathering on and on about your divorce and your ex.

Let me give you a concrete example of how someone I know did exactly that. The first holiday season after my divorce was final, I went to a Christmas party hosted by some friends. This party was a big affair, and it brought together a lot of people from many different circles. The couple who hosted it had invited people from past and present jobs, their college days, their gym, their church, their kids' schools—you name it. The guest mix was such that everyone was assured of not only running into friends but meeting new people, too.

I spotted an acquaintance I'll call Kim in the opposite corner of the room. I knew Kim and her husband had split up not long after That Man and I did, and I had heard through mutual friends that the divorce had gotten pretty contentious. Not only was I glad to see Kim there, I was encouraged to see her chatting with people I didn't know. I thought it was a good sign that she was getting out and socializing—a necessary step in moving on. I worked my way over to her to say hello. This was a decision I would quickly come to regret.

As soon as I entered the conversation, one participant used the opportunity as an excuse to go freshen his drink. When I glanced at the faces of the other two, I quickly noticed their glazed-over eyes, which told me the listeners had checked out of the conversation—or rather, the one-way tirade—a long time ago. Kim quickly greeted me and then immediately returned to her monologue. It was a blow-by-blow description of her divorce, complete with painful details about exactly how terrible it was and a side report on what a complete jackass her ex-husband was. Merry Christmas!

Kim went on and on. And on. And *on*. One person regained consciousness and tried to change the subject, but Kim wasn't having it. Another tried to empathize by sharing a divorce horror story of her own, but Kim also shut her down. No one's ex-husband was as big a jerk as Kim's ex, no one's divorce was as bad as Kim's, and no one's lawyer was as terrible as Kim's. After listening for about ten minutes or so, I managed to extricate myself and seek refuge in another room, where I found a more festive group to join. (And truthfully, *any* conversation—even one about tapeworms—would have been more festive.)

About an hour later I passed through the living room again, and there Kim was in the exact same spot, still griping about her divorce to three different glazed-over guests. I felt sorry for them, but not as sorry as I felt for Kim. Here she had a fantastic opportunity: She was at a Christmas party in a house full of fun people, many of whom she didn't know—all potential new friends for the next chapter of her life. But rather than seizing this opportunity to move forward, she tried her hardest to pull everyone she met directly into the divortex of her past. She didn't even give herself the chance to dig into the cookies and eggnog. What a waste.

Whatever you do, don't be like Kim. Anyone who has been through a divorce already knows it can be a grueling ordeal. So, skip trying to convince everyone that yours is the absolute worst. When you meet new people or enter new situations, use them as a lifeline to a new future, not a tether to your past. Here are some pointers to help in that exercise:

- **Have preapproved conversation topics.** Protect yourself from defaulting into a conversation about your divorce by having "go-to" topics of conversation at the ready, such as current events, books, movies, sports, or travel.

- **Don't talk about your kids.** Although your children are lovely (and I really mean that), try to keep conversation about them to a minimum, too. The reason for this is twofold. First, a conversation about your kids can turn into a conversation about your divorce before you even know it. Second, in this period of rediscovering you, I want you to really focus on what your interests are as an individual, separate and apart from your role as mother.

- **Let other people talk.** Bringing up topics such as the ones I suggest above (current events, books, movies, etc.) encourages an exchange of opinions rather than a monologue, and it helps to keep you from talking only about yourself. Be sure to ask them questions, too, and then listen to their answers. The give-and-take of listening and talking, and the exchange of information that goes with it, are the building blocks of new friendships.

Taking good care of yourself, accepting invitations from friends, looking for opportunities to do new things, and making friends with new people when you get the chance will make steering clear of the divortex much easier. Plus, all of these things together will help to create the foundation for your new normal life. At first, all this will take conscious effort and will likely feel more like work than anything else. But before long, it will not only come naturally, it actually will be fun. That's when you'll know you are far enough away from the divortex to be safe from its pull. And don't forget to mark that date on your calendar.

PART THREE:

EXTREME MAKEOVER–
REPUTATION EDITION

10.

Spin Class
(Managing Your Message While Nursing Your Wounds)

The emotions that come at the beginning of your divorce—including fear, sadness, and numbness—tend to cause paralysis and depression. As time passes, these paralyzing feelings recede and others, such as anger, euphoria, and sometimes even a desire for revenge, take their place. There is nothing wrong with this transition in and of itself. In fact, it even counts as progress. You are turning a corner of sorts. But anyone who has taken driver's education knows that there is an increased risk associated with this maneuver. You could turn the wheel too hard and lose control. You could be going too fast as you approach the turn, causing you to career off the road or roll your vehicle. To avoid getting into a wreck, it's critical to be alert, focused, and disciplined when you execute this turn.

Anger is an emotion that tends to lead to acting out and euphoria is an emotion that tends to lead to going out. And acting out and going out can lead to big trouble during your divorce. Because you and your ex are suing each other over both the division of your property and the division of your children's time, your behavior is subject to intense scrutiny. Acting in a way that appears irresponsible, inappropriate, or antagonistic can have a negative impact on your case, leaving you with both less money and less time with your kids. So, at the exact time that you are likely to act inappropriately due to poor judgment, you're also more likely to be caught and suffer negative consequences as a result.

It's important to have strategies in place to help you manage your reputation. Otherwise, you might create messes that damage your position and take time and money to clean up. The guidelines in this chapter will ensure your behavior is above reproach.

Follow the two-sentence rule. Because people love juicy gossip and apparently have nothing better to do, you will be queried about how your divorce is going by folks who have no business asking and zero need to know. And because you are not your normal, sensible self right now, you might find it surprisingly hard to resist the slightest invitation to spill your guts to people you have no reason to trust with your confidential and extremely juicy business. Although you don't have a duty to protect your ex's reputation, there's no reason to ruin your own by telling everyone about all the ways he's done you wrong. If someone asks why you are getting a divorce, it's fair to say he was having an affair, if that's what really happened. But when you're at the library checking out an entire row of self-help books, don't hold up the line by telling the librarian how your ex was sexting with his hot yoga teacher. It's true this information may establish that your ex was a tool, but blathering on about it makes you look like a fool. (And if you see yourself in this last example, as soon as you've checked out your books, be sure to check in with your therapist. Oversharing with strangers about your divorce is a sure sign that you're overdue for a session.)

The two-sentence rule is the best defense against saying too much when someone other than a close friend asks you how your divorce is going. Have a two-sentence answer scripted, rehearsed, and ready to go. Your answer should be something like, "It's been hard, but I'm getting through it. Thanks for asking." Then, when a casual acquaintance or a not-so-close friend asks you what's going on, you will know exactly what to say. Recite your two sentences and quickly change the subject by asking them a question ("How are things with you?"). Following the two-sentence rule to avoid saying too much to anyone other than your A-Team will go a long way toward protecting your reputation from self-inflicted wounds.

Don't have an egg on your Facebook page. The first place your ex's divorce lawyer is going to look for embarrassing evidence to use against you is your social media accounts, such as Facebook, Twitter, and Instagram. Even if you think your privacy settings are tighter than your ex was with money, you must assume that everything you say on social media will be read by everyone—including your ex and his lawyer. This means you should never, ever dish about your divorce, make snarky comments about your ex (no matter how true), or post photos of you and your BFFs doing Jello shots at Coyote Ugly. No matter how liberating it feels to post those pictures at 1:30 AM, you will only feel humiliated at 1:30 PM when you are answering deposition questions about the episode. And if you are fighting for custody, you just bought your ex a round of evidence.

It's not just what you write on your own page that can be scrutinized; any comment you make on anyone else's page is also fair game. Plus, any remarks your friends post about you can also come into play. Sometimes the most troublesome comments are from well-intentioned friends who are simply trying to be supportive: "Hey! Saw your ex-husband in the mall parking lot with some ho bag. I guess that's his new monster truck? It's so subtle! No one would *ever* guess what he's overcompensating for." Or "Missed you at happy hour on Friday! Ran into that former student of yours there. He asked where you were. I think he's hot for teacher." Whether these statements are true or not isn't the issue. They create an impression of you and what you're saying and doing, and you may have to answer for all of it.

Because there are so many ways to go wrong, most lawyers advise their clients to shut down all social media accounts until their divorce is final. That is undoubtedly the most foolproof approach. Short of that, you can maintain your accounts but restrain yourself by acting as if you have "view only" privileges. In other words, you can get on Facebook, Twitter, and Instagram *only* to see what everyone else is saying and doing, but not say a single word yourself. If you take this approach, your first order of business should be to change your Facebook page to get rid of your wall. This will eliminate the possibility of people posting comments that might be inappropriate. If friends want to tell you something, they can either message you or do it the "old-fashioned" way—call or send you an email.

Crazy isn't your best color. Your ex's number one objective right now is to convince everyone that you are completely crazy. (And since divorce doesn't bring out the best in people, that can be remarkably easy to do.) Your number one objective is to make sure you don't provide him with a paint-by-numbers sketchpad and a fresh supply of paint. Don't set his classic rock album collection on fire in your front yard, giving a new meaning to Blue Oyster Cult's anthem "Burnin' for You." Don't drunk-dial him and leave crazy messages on his cell phone in the middle of the night. Don't secretly attach a GPS tracking device to his car, even if you're sure that he's been cheating (and it turns out you were totally right).

All these actions will only make you look crazy, which in turn will make his jerky behavior appear somehow justified and put you on the defensive. The narrative will change from one in which you're struggling to do your best to make it through your divorce to one in which you're the crazy wife who eventually drove him to leave. ("Sure, he ran out on her. But who can blame him? She's *crazy*!")

Don't buy yourself problems. Every dime you spend will be subject to scrutiny during your divorce. You will be required to provide copies of all your bank account and credit card statements to your ex, and all your spending will be carefully reviewed. That means every time you make a purchase while your divorce is pending, you are buying a conversation piece for your ex and his lawyer.

Be mindful of the picture you are painting. Charges on your credit card statement to spas, clothing boutiques, bars, and expensive restaurants create one image, and charges to grocery stores, bookstores, movie theaters, and kid-friendly pottery painting studios create quite another. You don't have to live as if you've taken a vow of poverty, but you should live within your budget so you don't buy yourself more trouble.

In addition to the picture you create for your ex and his lawyer through your spending records, keep in mind how your spending choices make you come across to people in general. If you sell your minivan and buy a brand-new Camaro, you've just swapped your reputation as a soccer mom for that of a floozy. That's a bad trade. Also, it's one thing to update your wardrobe, especially if you've dropped a lot of weight and your current clothes don't fit you anymore, but don't buy a bunch of new clothes that scream "cocktail waitress" (unless you *are* actually a cocktail waitress).

Don't manufacture evidence against yourself. Protecting your reputation during your divorce isn't rocket science. Not interested in answering embarrassing deposition questions about your sex life? Then don't have a sex life. Don't want to read letters from his lawyer telling your lawyer that you need to stop texting your ex at 2:00 AM? Then don't text your ex at 2:00 AM. Not looking forward to explaining what you and your kid's smoking hot tennis coach talked about for an hour on your cell phone late Saturday night? Then don't talk to your kid's tennis coach for an hour on your cell phone.

I understand you might really, *really* hate your ex right now. I'm not saying you have to somehow magically or instantly get over it. But you have to make sure that you don't let your anger double-cross you and start working as a double agent. Every chance you get—which is pretty much every minute of every day—I want you to make the conscious choice to be better and smarter than your anger would have you be. Use your anger to fortify, rather than weaken, your resolve to avoid making mistakes that will benefit your ex.

Keep out of trouble. The best way to keep out of trouble is to stay occupied with constructive activities. Find friends who are game to do things with you, but make sure to stick with your reasonable friends rather than the ones who have an appetite for drama. If you are taking a cooking class with someone on your A-Team, that's one night you won't spend obsessing over whether things are getting steamy between your ex and his spicy new administrative assistant. If you are on a walking tour of historic homes in your neighborhood, you won't be on a self-guided tour of your ex's new neighborhood that involves driving past his house again and again. Not only do positive activities distract you from thinking about your ex, but also they lay a healthy foundation for your new normal life.

Get a job. If you don't have a job, consider getting one. Although starting a new job can be stressful, it is an instant game changer and one of the best ways to turbocharge your effort to move past your divorce. Going back to work will require you to adjust to a new routine, learn new processes, and interact with a whole new crowd of people. All of the time and energy you spend doing those things will be time and energy you won't be spending thinking about your ex. Additionally, going back to work conveys that you are doing all you can to accept your new reality and move forward in a constructive way, and that plays really well with judges and juries.

Get a cause. There's nothing like volunteering for a real charity to make you feel less like a charity case yourself. Getting a close-up look at other people's troubles helps you to keep yours in perspective. Spending a few hours at the food bank helping to bag groceries for the hungry will teach you that viewing your divorce as the world's biggest problem is a "Let them eat cake" kind of attitude. A regular shift at the homeless shelter will put to bed any notion that your struggle to divide one household into two is a bigger problem than not having a home at all. Like exercising, volunteering helps you look and feel great. Plus, you're making the world a little bit better in the process. All of that adds up to win-win-win.

Don't lose custody of your sense of humor. I realize that divorce is more of an ass-kicker than a thigh-slapper, but there is huge therapeutic value in laughing. When your ex accidentally texts you—instead of his yoga teacher–turned–latest-girlfriend—that the house key is under the mat and he's in bed waiting, rather than letting that wreck your mood, have some fun imagining how badly out of alignment his chakras will be when he figures out his mistake. (And also be grateful that you no longer have to share a house with that downward-facing dog.)

Make sure to share these lighter moments with your A-Team. They have to do a lot of heavy lifting when it comes to your divorce, so don't forget to treat them to some levity, too. There's nothing like a shared laugh to keep all of your spirits up. Having the ability to laugh has a tremendous impact on how you come across to everyone—from your friends and family to the cashier at the supermarket. Laughing helps to part the storm clouds that are hovering over your head and let a little sunshine in. And everyone looks better with a little sun.

Use the headline trick. Here's a foolproof trick that can help you double-check your judgment at any given time. Let's say you see your neighbor as you're pulling into the driveway at the end of the day. He's divorced himself and has a couple of kids who go to school with your kids, but his children are with their mom for the evening. He asks you to grab a quick glass of wine. He is friendly and normal and this wouldn't be a date, just a couple of neighbors having a quick drink. Your six-year-old son and ten-year-old daughter are with you.

Your first instinct is to say no. After all, it's a school night and you don't have a sitter. Your neighbor suggests you just pop in a DVD of their favorite movie, *Despicable Me*, and the two of you will zip over to the closest place with a full bar, TGI Fridays. You've never been to that restaurant before, nor have you ever left the kids at home alone. But the notion of having some adult conversation over an adult beverage sounds pretty good. And it's only 6:00 PM and it's not as if you'd be gone long. The whole idea is surprisingly tempting.

To figure out whether this is a good idea or not, imagine something going wrong while you're gone, like a house fire. Then imagine how the headline would read in the paper the next day: "Firefighters Rescue Two Children from Burning Home. Mom at TGI Fridays Having Drink with Neighbor."

Now the answer is crystal clear, isn't it? Leaving your kids home alone while you grab a drink with your neighbor isn't worth it. It puts you in a bad light as a mother and provides your ex and his lawyer with all kinds of fodder to use against you. If that's not bad enough, no one would ever again trust your taste in restaurants once word got out that you went to TGI Fridays.

Consider another scenario: Your boss asks you to stay late to work on a project, but you need to pick up your kids. You consider calling your neighbor and asking him to pick them up along with his, and then letting your kids hang out at his house until you can get home. But you've never done that before and you are on the fence about whether it's a good idea.

Once again, use the headline trick to figure out the right answer. Imagine that your neighbor has a car accident on the way home from school. The headline the next day would read something like this: "Car Accident Sends Driver to the Hospital. Four Children Are Fine." There's nothing scandalous about that. Your neighbor was driving the kids home. You were at work. No juicy details, no questionable judgment. No substandard restaurant choices. You're good to go!

The headline trick can help you arrive at sensible answers even after your divorce is final. If you would feel embarrassed to read about the situation in the newspaper, or if there is anything about it that seems questionable or makes you defensive, then it's probably a bad plan.

Don't be a victim. Almost as damaging to your reputation as being a stalker or a floozy is coming across as a victim. Although you don't want to initiate or take the bait when it comes to pointless fights, it's also important to stand up for yourself on substantive matters. Standing up for yourself is essential to your own sense of self-respect, too. It influences how your children perceive you. It affects your friends' and family's opinion of you. And it establishes the ground rules for your post-divorce relationship with your ex.

If your ex tends to take advantage of you or bulldoze over you to get his way, it's incumbent upon you to put a stop to that. It may not be either productive or economically feasible to battle these points out through your lawyers every time, but that doesn't mean you should do nothing. Make adjustments to how you handle things going forward so you don't get plowed over again.

My ex used to suffer from a raging case of favor amnesia. He would ask me for a favor, such as trading weekends with Hannah. Because I was concerned about not being portrayed by him as the stereotypical bitchy ex-wife, and because I am a naturally agreeable person (no, really!), I would routinely grant his requests. But when it came time for him to return the favor, he would completely forget the fact that he actually owed me one from the time before.

My sister Angela got really fed up with my repeatedly falling for this routine and one day, after listening to yet another installment of this same story, she demanded, "How many times are you going to let this happen?"

"Let what happen?" I asked.

"Let your puppy get eaten by his alligator!" she replied.

I sat there quietly, trying to make sense of the sudden plot twist in our conversation.

"It's like you keep bringing a cute little puppy to show-and-tell while the class bully keeps bringing an alligator. Every single time his alligator eats your poor little puppy. Not only should this *not* come as a surprise anymore, you're at fault for not protecting that little puppy because you know he's bringing an alligator. For heaven's sake, quit bringing a puppy to show-and-tell. Either bring an alligator or don't go at all."

When she put it like that, I saw her point. Because I was still thrown off by the divorce and was overly concerned with how I was coming across, I was repeatedly allowing him to take advantage of me. It was obvious to everyone but me. People grow tired of folks who keep letting themselves be victimized. If you aren't doing your part to protect yourself, before long your support team will begin to resent having to do all the work for you. If you want sympathy and support from your A-Team, your other friends, and your family, they have to see that you are also pitching in. It's a team effort.

The next time my ex needed me to swap weekends, I decided that I could either decline or insist that he give me the extra weekend up front, effectively requiring him to pay in advance. Whether I explained what prompted the policy change was neither here nor there. What mattered was recognizing the pattern and taking action to protect myself.

The first time you stand up for yourself, you might get some push back. But in most cases, it only takes a time or two before your ex realizes that he has to deal fairly with you if he wants you to be willing to deal with him at all. Having your ex learn that lesson about you is good for everyone—you, your kids, and him.

If at first you don't succeed . . . During my divorce, I was flipping through a magazine in my dentist's waiting room when a story caught my eye. It was a question-and-answer piece with a fitness guru. One question asked how people should handle it when they fall off the diet-and-exercise wagon. Her advice went something like this: When you get a flat tire, what do you do?

Do you change the tire and get back on the road again? Or do you grab a knife, get out of the car, and slash the other three tires and the spare?

I thought that advice was brilliant—and not just as applied to diet and exercise. No one gets everything right 100 percent of the time. Although your success rate counts, how you handle your failures matters at least as much and perhaps even more. You should never go into a divorce with the idea that the stress of it all entitles you to a meltdown or two, but you also shouldn't go into it expecting that you will behave perfectly, either. You are human. You will make mistakes.

When you realize that you have handled something in a less than ideal manner, own up to it rather than beating yourself up. Take an honest look at how you blew it. Try to pinpoint what triggered your poor judgment or bad behavior. Learn what you can from your mistakes so you can avoid making similar ones in the future. Then put them behind you and move on.

11.

Friend or Faux?

(Determining Who to Put on Your
Starting Lineup and Who to Bench)

When it comes to divorce, everything gets divided up: investments, debt, furniture, family photos, pets, and even time with the kids. What once was "ours" gets reclassified as "yours" and "mine." The details of the division are then memorialized in the divorce documents. He gets the NASCAR memorabilia; you get the Scentsy distributorship. He gets the dog; you get the cat. He gets the kids the first and third weekends of the month; you get them the second and fourth. You may not like either the exercise or the outcome, but at least you understand the drill.

There is one group of assets that is left out of the formal divorce process entirely: your friends. Because friends are a primary source of comfort and support (and there's nothing like a divorce to make you need heaping helpings of both), how this valuable group of assets gets divvied up can have a big impact on how well you bounce back.

In a perfect world, friends wouldn't have to take sides in the wake of a divorce. (And adorable Keebler elves *really would* bake delicious cookies in tree trunk bakeries!) But we don't live in a perfect world; we live in the real world. And here's another news flash: Although you don't have much say over which friends you get to keep after your divorce, you do have the power to drive friends away. Just try launching a campaign to convince them how terrible your ex is and see how fast your cell phone stops ringing.

It's up to your friends to decide whom they'll stay close to after your split. They know both of you and they'll make the decision that's best for them. If you find yourself getting irritated with certain friends for choosing your ex, try to think of it this way: You probably don't feel very sympathetic about your ex's emotional state at the moment, but, if you two have kids together, it's in their best interest that their dad not implode right now. And having the support of friends when experiencing something as stressful as divorce can go a long way toward keeping a person from cratering.

Resist the urge to lobby, and instead relax and let your friends figure things out for themselves. Once the dust has settled and your friends have decided who gets custody of their friendship, then there will be work to do. You'll need to evaluate the friendships you're left with, determine what category each one falls into, and proceed accordingly.

Model Friendships

Before we evaluate your different categories of friends, let's take a minute to go over the two basic models that friendships can take.

The Group Friendship Fund. The GFF model features friends who are bundled together. They all know each other and tend to travel in a pack. Sorority sisters and fraternity brothers are common examples. The group nature of this model yields rewards that compound daily. There's always a party somewhere, and, if you ever need an army of support, it's usually just one phone call away. The benefits of a GFF are never more obvious than when you have to move. With a GFF the heavy-lifting part of the move is over and you're all drinking beer and eating hot wings before you know it.

The rewards from this model can be big, but so are the corresponding risks. A person in a GFF is often reluctant to be honest with another friend in the same group out of fear that, if she says something that offends that one friend, the entire group might take sides. And if she ends up on the wrong side of group consensus, she could lose her entire social circle and have to declare social bankruptcy.

Another downside to the GFF model is that the importance given to the group as a whole leads to a lot of "group think," which in turn generates a lot of talking behind the backs of other members. Sure, the purpose of all this talk is ostensibly concern for the person being discussed or the need to determine the group's collective opinion of whatever matter is at issue, but it often ends up sounding (and feeling) more like gossip than concern, especially since all the talk rarely results in any group action.

I've seen "friends" in a GFF engage in a lot of hand-wringing and tongue-clucking about another member of the group who was drinking too much, having an affair, or otherwise making a mess out of her life. Everyone agreed someone should really talk to her about these concerns, but no one had the guts to do it. Instead, they all talked a lot *about* her, but not at all *to* her, as her personal and professional life circled closer and closer to the drain.

If you are in a GFF, you can typically expect a lot of support during your divorce—especially at first. Your friends are likely to turn out in force for you, helping you through the initial transition of either you or your ex moving out. But as your divorce progresses, there is a risk that your friends will collectively withdraw their support if they don't like how you are handling things. Rather than taking it up with you directly, and, without any heads-up, they begin to retreat. This retreat follows extensive discussions among themselves (but behind your back) about how you are mishandling this or that situation.

Losing an entire GFF during your divorce is bad timing, to say the least. You can lose an entire support network with little to no warning at a time when the emotional impact is magnified dramatically. This doesn't mean you should withdraw from your GFFs until your divorce is over. It means you should be mindful of the risks that are inherent with a GFF and make sure your friendship portfolio is diversified.

The Individual Friendship Account. An IFA is an individual friend who is not connected to your other friends. Think of IFAs as spokes on a wheel, with you as the hub. The advantage of an IFA is more opportunity for honesty on both sides of the equation. You can share things with an individual friend without being concerned that it will be broadcast to an entire group. If you give your honest opinion to a friend in an IFA and she gets mad at you, it may cost you that friendship, but you don't stand to lose your entire support system. This increased honesty means that stronger and deeper friendships tend to develop in an IFA than in a GFF.

The downside to IFAs is they take more effort to maintain and you don't get the compounding effect that a GFF offers. Catching up with five IFA friends takes five phone calls and five separate get-togethers. Catching up with five friends in a GFF takes one group text and a Thursday night happy hour.

There's also a rare but nonetheless serious potential risk with IFAs: You tend to feel at ease talking about one IFA friend to another friend because they do not know each other. It doesn't feel like gossip, but rather an opportunity for you to discuss your respective views of another friend's goings-on.

If those two friends later become friends themselves, the three of you are suddenly bundled together in a de facto GFF and any sharing you did in the past puts you in a precarious position. If those two friends compare notes, it could result in your being de-friended by both and exiled from the de facto GFF altogether.

I'm speaking from experience here. My friend Tessa was married to someone who was in a well-known band. Her husband was having an affair while he was on tour and, because I wasn't connected to anyone else in her life, she used to confide in me about the situation. I had another IFA friend, Allie, who was a chiropractor. I told Allie about Tessa and her struggles. I never gave any specifics such as names and addresses, but Allie knew I had a friend whose husband was in a band that toured a lot and that he was cheating on her. And because they didn't know each other, I was candid with Allie about my frustration when Tessa put up with stuff that I thought she shouldn't.

In a bizarre coincidence, Tessa ended up getting a job as a receptionist at Allie's office. Once she learned that Tessa's husband was in a band, it didn't take long for Allie to realize that she had heard this song before. Suddenly I was singing lead vocals without the benefit of any backup singers in the "friendship edition" of Justin Timberlake's "What Goes Around Comes Around." No one asked for an encore.

IFA friends make excellent A-Team members. Because they don't know each other, you minimize the risk of your innermost struggles becoming the topic of their group chat sessions. Also, the advice you get from IFA friends is more pure in that it has not been cross-contaminated by friends comparing notes behind your back. A downside to having two IFAs on your A-Team is that they do not have each other to turn to for support in the "helping a friend through a divorce" marathon.

So, which friendship model is better? As it turns out, it's a tie. An ideal friendship portfolio would be diversified, with one or two GFFs and a handful of IFAs. Whether your portfolio has a heavier concentration of one model than the other will likely depend on your personality—how outgoing you are, if you prefer depth to breadth, and your tolerance for risk.

Regardless of whether it's a GFF or an IFA, healthy friendships are a two-way street. In the normal course of things, there should be plenty of occasions to both give and receive support. If you notice that there is a historical imbalance on either the giving or receiving end of a friendship, take steps to correct it. If you find yourself burned out by a friend who is always a taker and never a giver, it's okay to withdraw your energy from that friendship and start investing in one that yields better rewards.

Putting Friendships to the Test

Here's a simple test to help you decide whether a friend is good for you to be around during this stressful time. Pay attention to how you feel immediately following an interaction with her. Is your mood better or worse than it was before the interaction? Do you hang up the phone and feel positive? Did the conversation boost your mood? Was your day just a little bit better because of it? Or, are you left feeling depressed, irritated, frustrated, or generally down?

I'm not saying it's everyone's duty to entertain or cheer you up every time you talk. And even positive friendships sometimes get out of step. But what you should be on the lookout for is "friends" who have subtle ways of making you feel bad about yourself during your divorce. They may not even be conscious of the fact that they're doing it—and you may not at first, either.

By making a note of how you feel in the immediate aftermath of a conversation with a friend, you can gain tremendous insight into whether this particular person is a positive or negative influence for you right now. Use the data to make informed decisions about whom you hang out with and how much time you spend with them when you do.

Friendship Categories

Once you have audited your friendship roster to determine how many GFFs and IFAs you have, the next step is to determine what type of friend each one is. The guide below will help you with this exercise.

Steady Edies. No question about it, Steady Edies are true friends. These are the people you can count on through thick and thin. They have always been there for you, and right now is no exception. It was from this ever-loyal group that you selected the members of your A-Team. The Steady Edies who didn't make the cut are still VIPs on your friendship roster. Because you have your A-Team on speed dial, you don't actually call your other Steady Edies at 2:00 AM when you're having an uncontrollable crying jag. But you could if you needed to, and you know they'd totally pick up the phone and talk you through it.

Crisis Junkies. These are parasites who live on other people's drama. And there's nothing like a divorce to bring Crisis Junkies out of the woodwork. Divorce is to Crisis Junkies what summertime is to ticks: It's their favorite season. The nastier the divorce, the more you'll find them crawling all over you.

The problem with Crisis Junkies is they are not hanging around out of genuine concern; they're using your hardship as an elixir for themselves. Your problems make them feel better about their own lives. And your dependence on their friendship makes them feel more important. Given this dynamic, Crisis Junkies are not rooting for you to get back to your even-keel self. They have a vested interest in keeping the drama going. Steer clear of Crisis Junkies during your divorce. You have enough to worry about right now without adding parasites to the list.

Fake Friends. They are acquaintances who want to buddy up to you during your divorce for one reason only: entertainment value. Divorce makes for juicy stories and that's entertainment gold. Not only can you *not* count on a Fake Friend to keep your confidences; you can actually count on them to betray them. After all, the payoff for having a juicy scoop comes when you share it.

In case you are having trouble determining whether a friend is a Fake Friend or a Crisis Junkie, here's an easy way to tell: Crisis Junkies don't mind logging in long hours with you during your darkest hours. In fact, they're happy to do so because those are prime parasite feeding opportunities. Fake Friends just want to get the story and run. If you're trying to figure out whether someone is a Fake Friend or a Crisis Junkie, save yourself the time and trouble. Either way, she is not someone you need to be associating with right now (or ever, really), so no further analysis is required.

Researchers. They tend to draw closer to you and ask a lot of questions during your divorce. Initially, you may confuse Researchers with Fake Friends, but there is a difference. Researchers are not in it for the gossip; they are in it for the information. They see you as the canary in the coal mine. Either consciously or subconsciously, Researchers sense that they themselves are dangerously close to divorce and they want to learn what to expect for future reference. You'll get lots of questions about how you knew for sure that your marriage was over, details of your financial arrangements, and how you spend your time now that you are living on your own. The problem with Researchers is that sharing information with them is like rolling the dice. They may not be gossips per se, but they may nonetheless be careless about repeating what you tell them because they see it as data rather than personal information.

Invisible Friends. These are people you thought were your buddies who have suddenly vanished. The loss of friends when you are going through a difficult time can be hard to take. The temptation is to conclude that they are siding with your ex or they have somehow abandoned you in your darkest hour. But the truth is you don't really know why these friends are MIA. Maybe it has something to do with your divorce, but maybe it doesn't.

I learned that the hard way, too. When I was going through my divorce, a friend I thought was a Steady Edie suddenly didn't want to have a thing to do with me. After a couple of attempts to reach out to her, I went on with my life, but thought less of her because she had bailed on our friendship at a time when I really needed support.

Months later, I found out what had really happened. At the time I was going through my darkest days, she had discovered that her husband had been acting like former Governor Eliot Spitzer—hiring expensive call girls and blowing through large amounts of their community cash. She was reeling in the wake of this discovery. Being a private person by nature, she reacted by retreating from everyone. She was an IFA, so I had no other friends with whom to compare notes. And because I was going through my own crisis, I assumed she was reacting to my drama rather than trying to survive one of her own.

As big as your problems feel right now, personal problems are not your exclusive domain. So, reach out to your AWOL friends if you want, but, if they blow you off, try to move on without reading into it.

Once you've assessed your post-divorce friendships and know who's who, tend toward the Steady Edies; keep the Crisis

Junkies, Fake Friends, and Researchers at arms' length; and gracefully let go of Invisible Friends. Remember, change is an inevitable part of life. And during your divorce, it's not just what's for dinner—it's for breakfast and lunch, too.

Diagnosing Divorceaphobia

Just as divorce causes you to reassess your friendships, it also causes others to reevaluate you. Don't be surprised if you encounter a group that judges you quite harshly—and without any legitimate basis. These people are suffering from a condition called divorceaphobia, which primarily (although not exclusively) strikes other married women who still have children at home.

Divorceaphobia stems from the drive to identify risks, determine the cause, and then quickly assign blame to everyone else's misfortunes. This is the same drive that might lead someone to ask whether a person was a smoker upon learning of his lung cancer diagnosis. In this way, people seek to reassure themselves that, as long as they do not make the same "mistake," they will not experience the same outcome.

As a general rule, there's no group on higher alert for risks than moms with kids still under the roof. Moms generally strive to protect their families against all threats. And divorce is widely regarded as public enemy number one. As a result, if a mom discovers that you are going through a divorce, it may trigger the onset of divorceaphobia. Symptoms may include a strong showing of fear, loathing, judgment, and scorn, and a surprising absence of caring or concern. Divorceaphobes often attempt to contain the threat they believe you pose by pigeonholing you into one of the following profiles:

Contagious Callie. Divorceaphobes who typecast you as Contagious Callie not only believe that divorce is a communicable disease but believe you are a carrier. Whether you were at fault for contracting it is irrelevant. The fact that you have it and it is contagious means they have to avoid you like the plague. Technically, you may still be alive, but socially you are as good as dead to them.

Sinner Sandy. Woe be to anyone who is labeled a Sinner Sandy. Divorceaphobes will not hesitate to cast the first stone—and they will continue to pelt you until you retreat completely from their sight. These moms don't need actual facts; they have already rendered judgment. You are guilty. God told them so. Plus, even if your divorce wasn't your fault (and they know it totally was), the mere fact that you are divorced makes you a sinner. Even though you may be hurting, don't expect any compassion from a divorceaphobe. They don't subscribe to that "soft on crime" New Testament nonsense. You're unclean, so it's straight to hell with no last supper for you.

Ball-Breaking Bianca. Even if you don't yet know exactly why your marriage unraveled, divorceaphobes have it all figured out. You were *such* a bitch to your husband! These moms know that the real question isn't why you're getting a divorce; it's how your husband put up with you as long as he did. It's obvious how pushy you are. You were so busy climbing up the career ladder you didn't even notice that your marriage was going down the drain. No one could expect a husband to live with the likes of you for very long—unless he's no man at all.

Frumpy Frances. You want to know why your marriage failed? Just look in the mirror. Those extra pounds and your plain Jane clothes? Two words: not hot. Husbands don't want to come home to someone who looks like you. It's no wonder yours struck up that affair with the new hire at his office. Divorceaphobes know the number one rule of affair-proofing your marriage is to never let yourself go. You broke the rule and now you're paying the price. You are now a cautionary tale that serves as motivational fuel to keep these terrified moms peddling as fast as they can while they sweat it out at the gym.

Being surrounded by divorceaphobes can make a bad stretch even worse. You are trying to get through one of the toughest ordeals of your life and suddenly you've become a social pariah and you have no idea why. I can solve the mystery for you. You are now a single woman—and one who is dropping significant chunks of weight thanks to the divorce diet. Divorceaphobes believe that a single woman who is getting thinner by the minute is a siren to happily married husbands everywhere. That makes you a direct threat to these women's marriages, no matter how amazing they insist they are. (And they always insist their marriages are amazing.)

Here's what you need to understand: If there was ever a time to bastardize a line from *Seinfeld*, now is the time: It truly isn't you; it's them. Moms who react to your divorce by demonizing you are operating from a place of fear. Although they might not realize it (and would never admit it even if they did), they are frightened about the health of their own marriages. But rather than taking an honest look inside their own houses, they'd rather make assumptions about what happened in yours instead.

Sadly, the only effective cure for divorceaphobia is for the divorceaphobe to experience a divorce of her own, which means her odds of beating the illness are fifty-fifty. Once you understand this, you'll know that it would be a waste of your time to try to convince them that you are not a threat to their marriages. Instead, enjoy the company of your Steady Edies and invest your energy in cultivating new friends.

That brings me to my final point on the topic of friendship during divorce. Over the course of your life, friends will come and friends will go. Don't fight the natural ebb and flow of this. Your friendship roster will undergo some change—and that's okay. Sometimes there's a specific reason; sometimes there isn't. Sometimes you know the reason; sometimes you don't. Instead of dwelling on the change or trying to guess the reason, remember what was good about that friendship and move on. Rather than characterizing it as a loss, view it as an opening on your roster for a new friend. Sometimes these friendships circle back around. Sometimes they don't. Either way, it's all good.

12.

Friends Don't Let Friends . . .

I have a present for you! It's nothing glamorous, but it is handy. It's a letter from you to your Steady Edies, with helpful instructions so they can know how to best support you during your divorce. Make as many photocopies as you have close friends, customize each letter by filling in the blanks, and then hand them out the next time you see them. Enjoy! And you're welcome!

> *Dear _____,*
> *Ever since we first met in/at _____*
> *back in _____, I knew we would be*
> *close friends. We've been through a lot together,*
> *like_____. And who can forget the*

time we_____? That was really
_____!

I don't need to tell you that what I'm going through now is one of the hardest things I've ever experienced. You've asked me how you can help, and I've given it some thought. Below are some ideas I've come up with.

Don't be a double agent. *There is a difference between providing support and picking sides. But having said that, it is also true that friends generally get divided up during a divorce. I'm okay with that because I understand that my soon-to-be ex and I both need friends we can trust. I'm counting you in my circle of support. But if I shouldn't, please tell me. I promise not to get mad at you. Letting me know that you are still close to my ex will keep me from oversharing with you about my divorce, and that will save you from being put in an awkward position.*

Assuming you do choose to be in my circle of support, please don't disclose any sensitive information to my ex in the event you run into him. I'm not saying you should give him the silent treatment when you see him. I'm just asking that you leave me and my life off the list of topics of conversation, even if you think that what you're saying puts me in a good light. Do say, "How's it going?" Don't say, "Your ex is hotter than ever. Guys are lining up to ask her out!"

Also, don't forget to tell me you saw him the next time we talk. That way, I won't hear about it indirectly ("I saw _____ with your ex at the car wash yesterday") and be left wondering whether you're straddling the friendship fence. I apologize if that sounds a little paranoid, but divorce is the leading cause of temporary insanity, after all.

Be a friend, not a judge. *People love to talk about other people's divorces—partly because they're juicy, but mainly because they're terrifying. People think that, if they can identify the reason and assign the corresponding blame, they can make sure that their marriage won't meet the same fate: She had an affair. He was impossibly demanding. As long as you don't do those things, your marriage should be okay.*

I'm not judging. I've done this myself. And this exercise actually has value to a point. Learning from other people's mistakes can be a good thing. But please make sure you don't inventory my faults and mete out blame in front of me. This is work for you to do for your own benefit—in private, or at least not in my company. What's done is done in my marriage, and I'd really appreciate your meeting me where I am now, not judging me for what happened in the past.

Give it to me straight. *If I am acting in a way that makes me look like an idiot or if I'm doing something that is detrimental to my children, my friends, or myself, please tell me. If I am leaning too hard on you and burning you out, let me know before you get to the point where you stop taking my calls. Even if you have gotten so sick of me that you never want to talk* *me again, for the sake of the friendship we used to have back when I was your sane, nondivorcing friend, please level with me first rather than just disappearing. In return, I promise I will not get belligerent, angry, or defensive. But if I do, just hand me this letter and point to this paragraph and I promise I will shut up.*

Try to keep your word. *Be there for me when you can, and when you can't I promise to understand. But please don't say you're going to be there and then not follow through. In regular life, when this sort of thing happens it's no big deal. People intend to do things, but daily life gets in the way. The problem for me right now is I don't have a daily life and I'm maxed out on rejection. I'm working hard to put a new life together and get back to my normal, thick(er)-skinned self, but I'm not there yet. So, if you think there's a chance that you won't follow through with a plan, please don't throw it out there.*

If you do make plans to do something with me— either at your initiation or mine—please try hard not to cancel at the last minute. Canceling plans with someone who is not in the middle of a major life crisis is not a big deal. But right now, while I'm trapped in this divorce hellscape, keeping busy is really critical.

Sometimes I view a night without my kids as a coveted break. Other times, it's a daunting block of time to soldier through. Either way, having plans fall apart at the last minute can be really depressing, es-pecially if the reason is something like, "I just need a night at home with my husband and kids." An excuse like that might be completely understandable among friends who are either happily married (like you) or blissfully single (as I will be in a few months' time). But to someone who is right smack in the middle of a divorce, that sort of statement can be like telling a homeless shelter that you can't show up for your shift at the shelter's Thanksgiving dinner because you simply have too much delicious food to prepare for your family's private Thanksgiving feast.

Just ask. *Divorce is an emotional roller coaster. Sometimes I'm devastated and other times I'm dancing on the grave of my dead marriage—and my answer can change from day to day, if not hour by hour. Rather than guessing how I'm feeling ("Are you just loving your new single life?"), a better approach is to simply ask how things are going. Try to avoid tones of extreme happiness ("Hey!! How the heck are you?!?") as if I had just won the lottery, or unimaginable despair ("How on earth are you holding up under the stress of this terrible ordeal?") as if a loved one had just died. If your inquiry into my well-being is a real invitation to tell you how I'm doing, I'll take it from there and fill you in.*

Catty stories welcomed! *If you run into my ex at a restaurant and he has some lettuce in his teeth or toilet paper stuck to his shoe, send me a quick text—or, better yet, a surreptitious photo. All those times you* *thought he was an insufferable tool when we were married but you had to keep your thoughts to yourself for the sake of our friendship? Well, now is the time for you to completely unburden yourself. Stories like these are pure therapeutic gold to me right now. The more, the merrier.*

I hope you don't think this letter is out of line. Your friendship has always been important to me. Now, it's more important to me than ever. My goal here is to protect our friendship, not run you off. I would never wish a divorce on anyone, but, if you ever find yourself having a rough time in the future, I promise I will be there for you just as you are here for me now. I hope for your sake I never have to make good on that promise, but I also hope that just knowing that I'm here for you, should you ever need me, at least gives you some peace of mind.

Love,

_____

13.

Your Post-Divorce Personality

Everyone faces challenges in life. Some challenges are of such a magnitude that they can prompt permanent change in an individual's personality. Serious illness. Job loss. Death of a loved one. Divorce is also one such challenge. It's okay for divorce to change you, but it's not okay for it to define you.

People are multifaceted, so it should take many nouns and adjectives to convey an accurate sense of a person. If I were to rattle off some terms that I think describe me, I would include the following: Writer. Mom. Relationship expert. Recovering lawyer. Vegetarian. Italian American. Hello Kitty aficionado. Post-divorce thriver. You are a lot of things, too. Take a moment to think of at least five words or phrases that describe you, other than being divorced. Then add "divorced" to the end of that list. When you think about yourself, make it a point to give all the characteristics plenty of weight rather than simply focusing on that last part.

I know that your divorce may be looming large right now, but how you view yourself affects how others see you. Because you have the power to shape your perception of yourself, you also have the power to shape how others perceive you. I am not suggesting you dismiss or deny the impact that living through a divorce has on you, but I am cautioning you against letting it take over your life.

The intensity of a divorce can cause you to slip into another personality temporarily. Your judgment may be off as a result, so you may not notice. That temporary change can settle in and become a habit, and if the habit sticks around long enough it can become second nature. Before you know it, your personality has permanently changed.

To the extent going through a divorce changes you, the goal is for it to make you better, not worse. So, if the personality change you've experienced is an improvement over your pre-divorce personality, then bravo. But if it is not, you need to correct course as quickly as possible.

There are five post-divorce personality disorders that commonly affect women, which I've profiled below. The tricky thing about these profiles is there's no telling who's likely to assume which personality. There's no pattern to it, such as Bad-Ass Barbara transforming into Stalker Stacy, or Calm Carla morphing into Runner-Up Rhonda.

Although you can't predict, you can prepare. Familiarize yourself with the following five profiles, and have your friends and family familiarize themselves with them, too. Then, if someone notices that you're starting to change, together you can spring into action and begin the appropriate treatment plan.

Train-Wreck Trina. Train-wreck Trina may be going through a grown-up life event like a divorce, but that doesn't mean she can't party like a sorority girl on academic probation. Train-Wreck Trina thinks the best way to prove to everyone else—but especially to her ex—that her divorce hasn't caused her to miss a beat is never to pass up a happy hour or a one-night stand. For her, divorce is a race against her ex to see who can recouple the fastest. And the finish line of moving on is moving in together.

What Train-Wreck Trina doesn't get is that replacing your partner without reviewing what went wrong with your last relationship sentences you to repeating the same mistakes. That's why rather than moving forward, Train-Wreck Trina ends up spinning her wheels.

The treatment plan for Train-Wreck Trina is a ramped-up social life that doesn't involve men. Think girlfriend trips, book clubs, training for a triathlon—anything to keep her busy, but out of bars and beds. That will help her to use the time between relationships to construct a healthy, independent life and give her the chance to sort out what went wrong with her last relationship before heading down the wrong track again.

Bitter Brittney. Bitter Brittney never wanted this divorce and she's not going to let anyone forget it. Her daily forecast is angry, with a chance of tirade. She systematically blowtorches every opportunity for a fresh start. Even when she meets new people, the first (and only) thing she wants to talk about is all the ways her no-good ex did her wrong. Her vibe is so toxic that she drives even her closest friends away. Because bitterness has become her baseline, Brittney has no way to gauge either how miserable she is or how insufferable she is to be around.

The treatment plan for Bitter Brittney is to establish a strict rule that forbids her from talking about her ex. She'll need to enlist help from her friends and family in this effort. To start, she should designate an alternative topic—such as movies or current events—and let everyone know what this substitute topic is. Then, when she finds herself wanting to talk about her ex, she or her friends can deliberately switch to the "go to" topic instead. Over time, this practice will retrain Bitter Brittney's brain so that her ex is no longer the only topic she'll discuss.

Stalker Stacy. Stalker Stacy has split up with her ex, but monitoring him is still her full-time job. And when it comes to stalking, she definitely has skills. We're not talking about a low-tech operation involving driving by her ex's house morning, noon, and night—that's for beginners. She takes full advantage of today's technology, hacking into his credit card and email accounts so she can track all of his activities and interactions. Oh, and you know that GPS feature on cell phones? Well, her ex never thought to turn his off. Since she still knows the password to his cell phone account, she can log in and clock his every move. Stalker Stacy is so consumed with secretly monitoring her ex that she has neither the interest nor the time to make plans with anyone else.

For Stalker Stacy to get back to her regular self, she needs a new hobby—something with intensity that will both occupy her time and get her adrenaline pumping. A consuming new pastime like hunting either ghosts or game will break her habit of chasing her past and tracking her husband.

Runner-Up Rhonda. Sure, her husband dumped her for his hot administrative assistant, but Runner-Up Rhonda still has "first wife" status. She knows deep down that her ex just can't live without her. After all, he needs her to pick up his dry cleaning, print out the kids' weekly schedule, and send a card to his mom on Mother's Day. (She even signed his name and everything!) She knows she's still a VIP in her ex-husband's life. What she doesn't get is that the "P" stands for prisoner, not person—and she's her own jailer. Because of all the errands she runs for her ex, she doesn't have the time or energy to establish her own post-divorce life.

The problem with Runner-Up Rhonda isn't her ability to give; it's the person to whom she's giving. To return to her normal personality, Runner-Up Rhonda needs to find a new beneficiary for all of her nurturing energy. Volunteer gigs such as spending time at a children's shelter or signing up for regular shifts for Meals on Wheels are good ways to indulge this tendency while moving forward with her own life, rather than trying to keep her place in her ex's life.

Victim Valerie. Victim Valerie wants the world to know that she's still hurting over her divorce. She uses Facebook as an outlet to share messages about healing, the precious nature of true friendship, the sacred value of women, and how it's not your fault when mean people hurt you—it's theirs. What Victim Valerie needs to realize is that being a victim is supposed to be a temporary condition, not a permanent identity. And although her friends were truly sorry for her at first, the "sell-by" date of their sympathy has long since expired.

Victim Valerie needs to pull the plug on her pity party. This requires putting herself in a position of power so she can begin to see herself in a different light. She doesn't have to run for governor (unless she's game, of course), but she should pick something in which she has interest and expertise, and spearhead a project in that area. From coaching a youth basketball team to leading a Girl Scout troop to serving as an officer in her neighborhood association, it's not the project that matters, it's the capacity in which she serves. By volunteering to lead an effort, Victim Valerie will see herself as someone who has the power to make good things happen, not someone who sits by powerlessly while bad things happen to her.

By catching these personality transformations early and instituting corrective measures as soon as possible, you can be assured of not just returning to your old self, but becoming You 2.0—a better version of who you were before your divorce. And there's a name for that girl, too. It's Healthy Helen.

Healthy Helen. Although Healthy Helen doesn't seek out rocky roads, when she finds herself on one she doesn't stall out—she drives with both hands on the wheel. She's in charge of where she's going, but she's not afraid to admit when she makes a wrong turn. She owns up and learns what she can while always moving forward.

It is hard to see these changes while they are happening to you, so it is essential for you to give your A-Team full permission to help steer you back on course at the first sign that you are going negative. It helps to designate a safe word in advance—something like "crazy train"—for your friends to use when they see you morphing into someone else. Agree up front that if they promise to have the guts to call you on your negative personality change, you promise not to get mad at them. Then it's up to all of you to keep your word.

14.

Keeping Things with Krystal Light
(How to Deal with Your Ex's Next)

However happy you are to be out of your hellhole marriage, and however thrilled you are that you no longer have to put up with your ex anymore, coping with his new love life can nonetheless test your sanity almost as much as being married to him did. You're acting like a responsible grownup: You're waiting to date until your divorce is final so you can focus on helping your kids through the transition, and you're committed to figuring out your part in what went wrong with your relationship before you dive into another one (which you'll tackle in Chapter Eighteen: Checking Your Rearview Mirror). Of course, none of this means that your ex is taking the same mature approach. And if he's not, he's likely to have a lot of turnover in

his post-divorce love life, and that can result in a bumpy ride for
your kids.

I'm speaking from experience here. In the years since my
ex and I split up, he has been through more than a couple of
relationships—and there have been other romantic misfires in
between. Although there's a lot of downside to the frequent
turnover in his love life, there has been one distinct advantage:
It has given me an opportunity to conduct firsthand research
on the dos and don'ts of interacting with the "next" of an ex
(who, for the sake of convenience, I'll refer to as "Krystal").
I've pooled this research with the data I've gathered from other
women who have been in this same position, and I've developed
some pointers to keep you from having to reinvent the wheel.

It's frustrating to watch your kids get buffeted by the turbulence created by your ex's love life, but yours is a sideline seat
and there's only so much you can do to improve the situation.
It's important to have a clear understanding of the limits to your
power so you don't end up doing things that do not help, or
reacting in a way that makes the situation worse.

Don't give your kids the third degree. Asking your kids questions about their dad's love life or his girlfriend (or girlfriends)
puts your kids in a terrible position. Maybe you're just trying
to make small talk. Or maybe you're trying to make them feel
less awkward about the situation by signaling that you're fine
with the topic. But from their standpoint, the questions feel like
a trap.

Answering could make your children feel that they are betraying their dad by talking about his personal business. But de-
clining to answer could make them feel that they are defying or

snubbing you. They may also worry that by honestly answering your questions they could end up hurting you: If they like Krystal, that might make you feel bad, but, if they don't like Krystal, that might make you worry about them when they're with their dad. So, don't put your kids on the spot. If they want to talk about their dad's new flame, they will bring it up themselves.

Stay in the baby pool. If you and your ex have kids together, there will be times when you have to interact with Krystal. There are many reasons to keep things positive with her, but the biggest reason is this: For as long as Krystal is your ex's girlfriend, she will probably be spending a fair amount of time around your kids. The last thing you want is for her to dislike you and either take it out on your kids or try to alienate them from you.

Your goal is to keep the conditions with Krystal exactly how you'd want them in the baby pool: shallow, warm, and sewage-free. When circumstances require you to interact with Krystal, you don't have to act like her new best friend. Remember, insincerity is easy to detect—especially for your kids. If she is around for any length of time, you will get to know her gradually. There's no need to either fake it or push it. Don't be overly friendly, but don't be an ice queen, either. If you have to interact with Krystal, it will most likely be at an event that involves your kids. Acting overly frosty only makes your children uncomfortable and threatens to make the event awkward. Be cordial. Keep the conversation short and the tone pleasant.

Don't overreact. If your kid comes to you with a complaint about Krystal, your job is to listen and not overreact. When you overreact, it shuts the conversation down and makes it less likely that she will come to you with a similar concern in the future. Your kid didn't bring up the topic so she could hear you go on a rant about your ex or his girlfriend; she brought it up because she has something to say. And you want your kid to feel free to come to you when things are on her mind. The more you listen and the less you react, the easier it is for her to talk. Then, in the course of this conversation, you can help her think through how to handle the situation.

Focus on what's best for your children. Chances are, your kids will like some of their dad's girlfriends and dislike others. When it comes to a girlfriend they like, don't be surprised if you find yourself wrestling with feelings of jealousy—not because your ex is into her, but because your kids are. In this situation, you have to remember that this isn't a popularity contest between you and Krystal in which your kids each get a vote. You are not in high school (though Krystal may be close to it, age- or maturity-wise). Given that your kids are going to spend time at their dad's house, it's better and healthier for them if they aren't miserable when they're there. If his girlfriend adds stability and makes the time pass more pleasantly, then that's to your kids' benefit.

It could also work out that you like Krystal, too. In that case, you might find yourself feeling conflicted over what's best for your kids and what's best for her. When you're thinking of your children's best interest, you want the relationship to last because she improves the situation for them at their dad's house. But if you're rooting for her, you want her to wise up and get out while she can. Again, your job is to put your kids first. Unless Krystal specifically asks for your opinion, it would be out of line to offer it. (And in my personal experience, she never comes to you for advice until after they break up.)

If you compete, you lose. Girlfriends come and girlfriends go, but moms are forever. You and Krystal have completely different roles. She is your ex's current girlfriend. You are your children's mother. You and Krystal are not in competition with each other, so don't frame it that way in your mind. (And if she tries to frame it that way, do not fall for it.)

If you create or get sucked into a competition with your ex's girlfriend, you automatically lose. You lose because you end up spending time and energy battling her, and those are resources you could be putting into something worthwhile. You lose because you end up modeling immature behavior to your kids rather than showing them how to move on with your life instead. And you open the door to your kids either getting used in the battle or caught in the crossfire, which puts them in a bad position. In short, nothing good can come from getting into a battle with Krystal, but a whole lot of bad sure can. So keep a clear head and enjoy your permanent role as your kids' one and only mom.

Don't lose sight of what matters. If you catch yourself obsessing over your ex and his new girlfriend, stop wasting your time. There are plenty of important things to think about, including making the best life and home for you and your kids. Focus on creating a life that is full of quality time together—time that is not interrupted by thoughts of your ex and his new girlfriend. Make your home a warm and loving place to be, not a lecture hall dedicated to a never-ending symposium on why your ill will toward your ex is justified.

You are in a great place. Your marriage is mercifully ending, and whatever happens between him and any girlfriend should not affect your quality of life whatsoever. You no longer have to put up with his nonsense. You have worked hard to escape your prison cell. Don't let Krystal lure you back in.

PART FOUR:

BETTER, SMARTER, STRONGER

15.

Remixing Your
Post-Divorce Soundtrack

(What to Do When the Message Goes Negative)

Imagine if bathing suits came only in size 16. Let's say you really wanted to go swimming, so you bought one of those bathing suits and put it on, even though you're actually a size 8. Then, after jumping into the pool, you had a serious wardrobe malfunction. Should that really come as a surprise to anyone? Would it be at all fair to blame yourself for this?

Marriage is like a size 16 bathing suit. For some people, it's a perfect fit. For others, it's a good enough fit. But for tons of people, once they take the plunge they find it doesn't fit right at all. To the extent there's outrage, it shouldn't be over how often this happens. The outrage should be over the fact that there is only a "one size fits all" option that doesn't work for most people, but no one is willing to address this.

I understand and appreciate the historical importance of marriage. In days of yore, trades were passed down from generation to generation. Tailors and cobblers taught their crafts to their sons, who eventually took over their fathers' businesses. Farms were kept in families for decades or generations. With this system a partner for life was a necessity.

Husbands were responsible for tending to the chores associated with either growing food or earning the money to buy food, and wives were tasked with the upkeep of the house. If all went according to plan, marital partnerships would yield a crop of children to provide additional hands to help lighten the load. Divorce would disrupt the family business model, which in turn could jeopardize the production and distribution of food and goods, and that would threaten the stability of entire communities.

Today, everything has changed. Most people get to choose rather than inherit their professions, and many folks change jobs or even careers several times over the course of their lives. Women now comprise nearly 50 percent of the American workforce and are the primary breadwinners in a growing percentage of American households, according to the latest data from the U.S. Labor Department. People are less likely to remain rooted in a geographic area, and the ability to move around has dramatically changed their relationships with their families. Also, the average lifespan has almost doubled since the 1500s, which means a lifetime commitment is a promise that could easily take twice as long to fulfill. Practically every aspect of our adult lives has changed, yet the way we formalize our adult relationships has acted like a stubborn spouse—refusing to budge. Not only is there just one model available, but the model itself has barely changed. Although it's true that couples who don't want to get married can simply date or live together, that's not the same thing as having a formal alternative to marriage; that's a choice between rules and no rules. In the United States, we are still deeply attached to the notion of having rules to govern our adult relationships. The degree of certainty provided by a set of rules gives couples the confidence to enter into joint endeavors, such as buying a house or having children.

I'm not suggesting that we throw the baby out with the bathwater. Traditional marriage has an important role in our society and I am not at all in favor of divorcing ourselves from it. I do believe, however, that we would benefit from another form of official partnership for adult relationships—sort of a "marriage light" option. Under this stepped-down arrangement, couples would form exclusive partnerships, but the commitment would last for a defined number of years rather than an entire lifetime. At the expiration of the term, a couple could either part ways or agree to renew for another term of years—or they could always choose the traditional marriage option.

Judging from the uproar caused by other efforts to modernize marriage, the idea of an alternative to marriage is likely to meet with plenty of resistance. It could take years or even decades before another alternative is available. But we don't have to sit idly by until then. In the meantime, we can at least get started on debunking the negative messages surrounding divorce. Because whether or not you agree that society would benefit from an alternative to marriage, I hope we can at least agree that, when it comes to divorce, the messages of failure are both unhelpful and unhealthy.

In this chapter we are going to examine the negative messages that may be reverberating in your head and record over them with some positive messages instead.

The Failure Fugue. One of the most common messages that women wrestle with as a result of divorce has to do with failure. If getting a divorce means you are a failure, then you're in good company. Roughly 50 percent of marriages end in divorce. These days, only 48 percent of American households are headed by married people—that's down from 78 percent in 1950, according to recent data from the U.S. Census Bureau. Given these statistics, rather than being surprised when people get divorced, we should question why we continue to raise girls to believe that marching down the aisle should be one of their top objectives.

It's not as if we give women permission to opt out of marriage altogether. Ask any woman in her thirties who has never been married and she'll tell you that the longer it takes to check this off her "to-do" list, the more probing questions she can expect regarding exactly what the problem is. In fact, a woman who marries and gets a divorce often has less explaining to do than a woman who has never gotten married at all. So, in the end, women are damned if they do and damned if they don't.

Most of us approach significant life events with good intentions and back up those intentions with planning and hard work. When a woman is pregnant, she does what she can to ensure she has a healthy baby. She reads books on pregnancy. She eats right and exercises. She rests. She gets the baby's room together. She may speculate about the gender and perhaps even get a sonogram to confirm her hunch. Nine months later she'll have either a girl or a boy. No one judges her for being right or wrong about her baby's gender. She's not a failure if it's a boy when she expected a girl. She doesn't have to defend or explain the outcome.

Marriage is like guessing the gender of your baby. You go into it with the best of intentions, but you have a fifty-fifty chance of getting it right. You try your best to make it work. You put effort, energy, and love into it. Then things work out however they work out. In your case it has worked out differently from what you anticipated. You thought your marriage would last forever, but now it is ending in divorce. That doesn't mean you're a failure; it means you're not a fortune-teller.

You may also be wrestling with a related theme: that your marriage itself was a failure. That's because the language that surrounds divorce is loaded with those negative messages. In fact, saying that a marriage "failed" is synonymous with saying that it ended in divorce. But there's a difference between a mission failing and a mission not going according to plan. The world wouldn't have chocolate chip cookies if things had gone according to plan back in 1930 when Ruth Graves Wakefield set out to make Butter Drop Do cookies, yet no one I know believes the invention of the chocolate chip cookie was a failure. To suggest that a deviation from what was expected at the onset of an endeavor can only be viewed as a failure is not rational. We don't hold other areas of our lives to this black-and-white standard, and we shouldn't do it with our marriages, either.

When you buy a house, you typically get a thirty-year mortgage. If you live in the house for ten years but then decide you want to sell it and move somewhere else, no one thinks that your first house "failed." When you decide to leave the job you've had since college and take another position somewhere else, no one views the first job you had as being a bust simply because you didn't stay there forever. That first house or job was likely good for a while, and then things changed. Maybe you grew out of the house and needed more space. Maybe the company you worked for got bought out and you didn't like the new management. But just because something comes to an end doesn't mean the entire thing was a failure.

Only you get to characterize the quality of your marriage. Whether your marriage had some great years before it got off track or was a train wreck from the very beginning is up to you to determine. Don't accept other people's attempts to label your experience. You were the one that was in your marriage. You are the one who is in a position to assess it.

The notion that either the husband or wife must die in order for a marriage to be labeled a success is as outdated as it is absurd. Just as a marriage that ends in divorce isn't necessarily a failure, a marriage that lasts until someone dies is not necessarily a success. Marriages are as unique as they are complex. You did the best you could with your marriage. Some things were within your control; others were not. No one knows better than you how hard you tried. Despite your best efforts, your marriage is ending. But just because you are not leaving your marriage toes up doesn't mean you can't hold your head high.

The Damage Ditty. Nothing has the power to cripple you like believing that you are permanently damaged goods as a result of your divorce. Believing this requires you to accept the faulty premise that being divorced somehow makes you an inferior person. You're smarter and stronger than that.

Getting a divorce is like breaking your leg. It's incredibly painful at first. In the initial aftermath it's really difficult to function. After your cast is removed, you have to go to physical therapy to get back your full range of motion. This creates a huge disruption in your life and it takes a lot of concentrated effort and hard work to get fully rehabilitated. But no one believes your broken leg will render you forever crippled. No one thinks you'll be in a cast or have to use crutches for the rest of your life. It's a temporary condition, not a permanent disability.

The same is true for divorce. It's one thing to recognize that you are not operating at 100 percent in the wake of splitting up, but it's another to believe you will never recover. There's no reason why you can't get better, unless you convince yourself that you cannot or you refuse to do the work that is required.

The "Has-Been" Hymn. Another variation on this theme is that you will be a "has been" after your divorce, with the best years behind you and nothing but loneliness ahead. Women who were cheated on, or have kids who are grown, or whose ex-husbands take up with much younger women are especially prone to this type of negative thinking. And if all three of those statements apply to you, you might be at risk of a triple dose of despair.

Whether you're twenty-nine or ninety-nine, your divorce doesn't represent the end of your story. It's just the end of a chapter—and chances are it wasn't all that great of a chapter, anyway. Even though this chapter may not have ended the way you wanted or expected, you now have an opportunity to begin another chapter—one with a fresh story line, new characters, and a different setting. Stop viewing your divorce as an ending and start thinking about what you want this new chapter to be about—and then start writing it. The sooner you start, the more time you'll have to develop the plot.

The Mortification Melody. Even though half of those who marry will go through a divorce, plenty of women still find getting divorced to be humiliating. Being embarrassed over your divorce is as counterproductive as it is illogical. All fifty states have a "no fault" approach to divorce, and you would do well to adopt a "no embarrassment" policy for yourself. If you got into a wreck and totaled your car, would it be reasonable for you to be humiliated? Would you decline the help of the firefighters who came with the Jaws of Life to get you out of the wreckage because it was all just too mortifying? Would it be healthy for you to let your embarrassment cause you to either permanently swear off driving, or refuse to take care of whatever is necessary to get mobile again?

Of course not. You would get out from the wreckage, get medical treatment, call a tow truck, file a claim with your insurance company, get a new car, and do whatever else you had to do until everything was resolved. Then you would get back on the road.

That's exactly what you need to do now. Cleaning up your life after something has gone wrong isn't embarrassing, but refusing to do so is. Don't give your divorce permission to disrupt your life in more ways than are reasonable. And don't forget that in many cases, getting a divorce is the best and bravest thing a person can do. If you manage your divorce responsibly, not only should you not be embarrassed about it, but you should actually be proud of it.

The Bitch Beat. You know the tired old stereotype: If you're a woman getting a divorce, that means you are a total bitch who is out to rob your ex blind. Fear of being typecast in this manner can make divorcing women bend over backward trying to be nice, and in the process they can end up allowing *themselves* to be robbed blind. It's called community property for a reason. It belongs to both of you. Standing up for yourself and insisting upon (and even fighting for, when necessary) your fair share of the community property does not make you a money-grubbing bitch. It makes you a responsible adult.

The Reject Refrain. Some women end up with this question stuck in their heads after a divorce: Who will want me now? This question affects your personal power the same way leaving your headlights on affects your car battery: It will drain you dry. When you allow your self-worth to be determined by whether men find you desirable, you give away power over yourself to other people—power that is rightfully yours. You have intrinsic value independent of whether other people find you datable. When it comes to your self-worth, your opinion is the only one that matters. That's why it's called *self*-worth. Rather than obsessing over what other people think, focus on being the kind of person *you* like and respect.

Worrying about whether anyone will want you after a divorce also reveals that you are already considering your next relationship when you haven't even finished extricating yourself from the current one. Using a new relationship as a way to medicate the pain of your last relationship is like taking a fistful of Oxycontin rather than going to physical therapy. It takes hard work to get better. You can't shortcut the process and expect to really heal.

The Done Wrong Doo-Wop. After experiencing betrayal or infidelity, some women croon about how they didn't "deserve" to be treated like that. The problem with focusing on the fact that someone did you wrong is that it keeps you in the role of victim. Even if your ex was a bully or a cheater or dumped you without warning, the quicker you can shift your thinking so that you view what he did as saying something about him (he was a jackass) rather than about you (you were his victim), the sooner you take back the reins of power over your life.

Of course, it's true you didn't deserve to be treated that way by him. But he did, and you were, and here you are now. Not only are you still standing, but you're holding your head high and you're moving on without him. There's an open road ahead of you and you're not going to take him with you by giving him free passage in your head. It may have been enough for Gloria Gaynor to survive, but you're taking things a step further: You're going to thrive. Where you're going doesn't have any room for guys like him. So, make sure you're not unwittingly bringing him along for the ride.

16.

A Tour of Your Future Hometown

In Chapter Seven I told you that going through a divorce is like trying to cross a river of sewage. The side you were on—the married side—was contaminated. You had to get to the other side of the river because that's where a healthy life awaited you. I explained that there was only one way to do this: You had to jump in and swim as fast and straight as you could, and not stop until you reached the other side.

You've been swimming like crazy! You've mastered day-to-day survival. You've slogged through significant amounts of the divorce nastiness with your lawyer. You've done your best to keep your communications with your ex to a minimum. You've been tending to the needs of your children as you shepherd them through this transition. You've been working on breaking out of the divortex. You've conducted yourself respectably. You've been taking good care of yourself. You've figured out who your friends are and you've manned your A-Team. You've made mistakes, but you've done your best to learn from them and move forward. And every once in a while when you've come up for air, you've caught glimpses of the land on the other side of the river as you've moved closer and closer to it.

Now, you've finally reached the other side. Way to go! That's a major accomplishment! I want you to stop for a moment, catch your breath, and admire the view. But then you'll need to get moving again because divorce recovery is a triathlon. Swimming through the river of sewage is the most grueling part—and you have that behind you—but you still have two more events to go.

The next segment of the triathlon is cycling away from the riverbank and toward the town inland where you will reside in the future. Of course you're going to reside inland. After all, no one wants to live on the banks of a river of sewage. The good news is that this stretch of road is not so bad. There will be areas where you'll need to pedal hard, but there will also be areas where you can coast a little, too.

In this chapter, we are going to take a visual tour of your new future—the one that you are getting closer and closer to calling home. It's a master planned community and you are in charge. Construction is definitely under way, but it is far from finished. Because everything is being custom-built, you have a lot of work to oversee. But things are starting to take shape already and it's obvious that the fruits of your labor are beginning to pay off. We are definitely getting closer to the fun part.

Your Bank

The first stop on the tour is your future bank. In case it looks smaller than you expected, that's not an optical illusion. It *is* smaller than your old one, and there's a reason for that, but you might not like it. Although the gap is getting smaller, the fact remains that most women drop income brackets after getting divorced. Simply put, you will most likely have less money than you did before, at least initially.

In light of this, the first thing you need to do is make sure you understand your new economic reality. Even if numbers are not your thing (and, believe me, they've never been mine), you need to be clear on how much you can spend in any given category. In other words, you need a budget. The second thing you need to do is actually stick to it. That means no spending sprees and retail therapy sessions.

If it is hard for you to find the self-discipline for your own sake, draw strength from an external source. Would you want your Patron Saint of Divorce to see you digging a financial hole for yourself and running up your credit cards? Or how about your own kids? Do you want them to see you making a mess for yourself (and them), or do you want them to see you acting like the grownup that you are? When your kids see you weighing the pros and cons of a purchase and saving up for bigger items (rather than putting them on a credit card before you can actually afford them), you are teaching them delayed gratification and financial responsibility. Those are much more valuable gifts than the huge, flat-screen TV you are tempted to buy to outdo the one at your ex's house.

If what's best for you and your kids isn't enough to keep you out of the mall and on the straight and narrow, as a very last resort consider this: Do you want to give your ex the satisfaction of seeing you make a mess of your financial affairs? If he is the type who always said that you would fail without him, don't prove him right at your own expense. You and your children will be the primary beneficiaries of all your efforts to manage your affairs well, but an unintended bonus will be proving that he was wrong about you all along.

Changing your spending habits doesn't mean you have to live as if you're under austerity measures for the rest of your life. But it does mean you'll have to make some lifestyle adjustments. I'm going to give examples based on assumptions I am making regarding your financial situation. Like all assumptions, mine will likely miss the mark a little in one direction or another. They will assume you have more or less money than you do. Don't get distracted by that. I'm not a carnival worker trying to guess your weight here. How much money you actually have isn't what's important. What *is* important is thinking through how to live well while living on less. These examples are intended to teach you certain principles so you can apply them to your own life.

If the examples I give paint a picture of a lifestyle that is above or below the one to which you are accustomed and you find yourself feeling either inferior or superior as a result, remember that unless you occupy the very last space on either end of the economic spectrum, there is always someone richer or poorer than you. So, pay attention to the principles, not the particulars. Now let's get to work.

Shopping. The first thing you need to consider is what's in it for you. If the emotional payoff is the thrill of buying, that indicates compulsive behavior and you need to find another pastime. But if you shop because you enjoy keeping your look up-to-date and you use rather than hoard what you purchase, then don't despair. Impulse buying at Neiman's may not be in your future, but you probably won't be forced to round up your wardrobe at Dress Barn, either. Plenty of women manage to keep their look current on a budget. Focus on the look rather than the label, find stores that offer what you want in a price range you can afford, pay attention to sales and coupons, and get on a store's email or call list so you can be alerted to markdowns. If that sounds like too much trouble, you can always take up sewing.

Eating out. This has long been one of my favorite pastimes. I love cooking at home, too. But going to a restaurant that has good food, interesting ambiance, and people who do the dishes afterward? That's every bit as effective as an hour on a therapist's couch for me—and cheaper, too. Plus, it never leaves a bad taste in my mouth.

Because eating out can really take a bite out of a budget, in the wake of my divorce I needed to figure out ways to cut back. Aside from the obvious, such as going to less expensive restaurants, there are several other tricks I've learned to help keep my restaurant tab from eating my lunch. Here are a few of them:

- Many restaurants have happy hour or after-hours specials featuring appetizer or small-plate menus for half price. Figure out which of your favorite restaurants offer these specials and time your dinner accordingly.

- Nothing bloats your bill like a bar tab. You can rein this in by having a glass of wine and an appetizer at home before going to dinner, or an after-dinner drink and dessert at home after you return. Feel free to invite friends and have them bring something, too—a bottle of wine, a carton of ice cream, whatever. Before you know it, you're not just going to dinner; you're enjoying a progressive dinner and saving money at the same time.

- Form a supper club with a few friends and take turns hosting. If the host provides the entrée and everyone else divides up the rest, the result is a dinner party without a lot of expense, pressure, or hassle. This can also be a great way of fortifying your post-divorce social life.

Travel. You can still satisfy your wanderlust, provided you're willing to make some changes. If you are flexible and creative, travel adventures are yours for the taking. Choosing less expensive destinations, staying in more modest hotels, taking road trips, and shopping travel websites for deals are all ways to make your dollars go further.

Despite a marked drop in income, I have had much better travel experiences post-divorce. I coordinate with friends or family, which minimizes expenses and maximizes fun. I stay in less expensive hotels because the best part of being on vacation for me is seeing what the destination has to offer beyond my hotel room. Sometimes I take my friends up on their offers to stay with them, which both allows me a chance to catch up with them and provides me the opportunity to see a city through a resident's eyes rather than a tourist's.

Though I took a greater number of trips when I was married, most of them (including all of the visits to my ex's old Boy Scout camp) were ones I didn't really want to take at all. And even trips to glamorous destinations such as Paris are no vacation when you're trapped in a bad marriage. But the very best thing about my post-divorce travels is that I no longer have a surly travel "companion," and that change alone makes all the difference.

Your expenses. Whatever your hobbies, make sure to keep your eye on the bottom line. Take a careful look at your monthly bills and credit card statements. Are you paying for things you are not using? I recently discovered that for the past two years, there's been an extra $9.99 charge on my monthly cell phone bill for a custom ringtone subscription I never once used and didn't even know I had. I'd also been paying for an individual gym membership even after my boyfriend had upgraded his plan to allow me to use his for free. Those two items alone resulted in savings of nearly one hundred dollars each month. That's not enough to retire on, but there are definitely other ways I'd rather spend that money.

If you think all these tricks are obvious, my response is this: There's a difference between knowing and doing. If you know your budget is tight and you are not doing any of these things to stretch your discretionary dollars, you are flushing money down the toilet. And if there's one thing you can't afford to do right now, it's to waste money.

Even though you have less money than before, a rich and wonderful life is still yours for the taking. Most people pay for more of everything than they truly need, and, for every pastime, there is almost always a more budget-friendly option available. Unless your hobby is bungee jumping, I encourage you to price-check your pastime and explore less expensive alternatives. You might even find that your satisfaction increases rather than decreases as a result. When that happens, feel free to thank me by using your savings to send me a reasonably priced bottle of wine.

Your Investment Firm

The next stop on your tour is your new investment firm. Your old one was housed in a bland office, with a lobby full of brochures featuring happy, silver-haired couples on vacation. That firm was exclusively focused on money, risk, and interest rates. Traditional investments are important, of course, but they aren't the most important ones. In your future, your investment portfolio is much more enriched, diversified, and enlightened—and that's why it looks more like a garden than a stuffy office.

There are many different kinds of wealth in this world. To have a truly balanced portfolio, you need to have a wide array of investments. Money cannot buy you happiness. In fact, it often comes bundled together with misery in a package deal. You've probably heard this before—and maybe you've even given lip service to it yourself. But the time has come for you to internalize this truth. Regardless of how large or small your monetary investments are, don't make the mistake of neglecting these other areas of potential wealth:

- health (physical, mental, and emotional),
- social well-being (including relationships with friends and family),
- intellectual and cultural enrichment, and
- spiritual nourishment.

Make it a practice to regularly audit how your investments are performing in each area. If you realize that you've been spending a lot of time with friends and family but neglecting your physical health by not getting enough exercise, make an adjustment. If you think you've been spending too much time watching TV and haven't read anything in six months, put down the remote and pick up a good book. You can compound your return by combining your investments: Set up a regular running date with a friend. Join (or start) a book club. With some conscious and consistent attention to each area of your portfolio, you will receive handsome returns. These investments can act as a buffer to keep hard times at bay and serve as a buoy when you do hit rough waters.

In case you think I'm just spinning some feel-good mumbo jumbo here, I'm not. Like most women, I dropped (several) income brackets after my divorce. I lost a lot of sleep worrying about my financial future and my ability to retire. But I worked with what I had and developed a balanced investment portfolio, and a wonderful thing happened: My overall wealth went through the roof. I am still in an income bracket well below the one I occupied when I was married, but I have never had a more rewarding life than I do today. I'm not saying this to brag; I'm telling you this to prove a point: If I can do it, so can you.

Your House

By now you've gotten the message: Bigger is not always better. There are some areas in life where size matters, but this isn't one of them. So, if your ego is at all tied to the size of your house, now is the time to let go of that once and for all. Such superficial attachments serve only to create roadblocks between you and real happiness.

A big, expensive house feels like a prison when you're trapped in a bad marriage. Granted, it's more like one of those country club prisons where they sent Martha Stewart, but, at the end of the day, jail is jail. My modest house is much smaller than the house I lived in before, and yet I love it so much more because it's a happy, loving place to be.

Your environment can have a big effect on both your mood and your behavior. Make sure to fill your house with things that sustain and enrich you, and get rid of things that radiate negativity or remind you of parts of your past that you want to put behind you permanently. Have you always thought a leopard-print rug would up your fierce factor? Now is the perfect time to go wild. Do you detest that deer head hanging on your den wall? Feel free to put it out to pasture. Do what it takes (within your budget, of course) to make your house reflect the new you.

Your Job

Most women have to work after their divorce. Many women always have, but others have to kick-start a career after years of being at home with kids. And some have to enter the workforce for the first time. Women often return to school to finish their degrees or pursue new ones. Even for those who have always worked, divorce creates the added pressure of knowing that you are now responsible for making sure a roof is over your head, the power is on, and food is on the table. Financially speaking, it all comes down to you.

When women are assessing their options in light of this new reality, they often feel obligated to get a job as quickly as possible. Many times, this leads them to choose a modest career—

one that might only take a year or less of additional school. In many cases, this ends up being a support staff position. There is nothing wrong with working in a support staff position if that's what you truly want to do. But if you've always wanted to be a CPA, don't accept the notion that you have to be a bookkeeper simply because of the years of education each job requires.

Make sure you think through all the variables. Do you enjoy school? How much is tuition? How much can you expect to earn from each position? Don't let additional years of school alone scare you off. If you manage your time right, the flexibility that goes along with being a student can result in a kid-friendly schedule. Particularly if you have been a stay-at-home mom and are now going back to work, spending a few years on a student's schedule can be a great way to ease through this transition for both you and your kids. When you consider all the factors, pursuing a career that involves more education may be the smarter choice in the long run.

Here's something else to watch for when it comes to choosing a new career: Everyone has a friend who has gone through rehab and then decided to become a substance abuse counselor. Or maybe you know a mom from playgroup who became so obsessed with childproofing her house that she decided to start her own baby-proofing business. In other words, sometimes people become so consumed by a personal transition that they mistakenly conclude they want to spend the rest of their professional lives helping to usher others through the same one. (I'll pause here for you to note the irony of this message being delivered by a woman whose own divorce inspired her to help other women navigate theirs. But again, I think my experience bolsters, rather than diminishes, my credibility.)

Sometimes those career decisions work out great. But sometimes people get a few years down the road, only to discover that they really don't want to have to think about those issues for the rest of their lives. It's just not where they are anymore.

If you find yourself wanting to get a degree in family and marriage counseling or go to law school so you can be a divorce lawyer, make sure you think this through carefully before you borrow a bunch of money and enroll in school for a counseling or law degree. Upon reflection, are you the type who has intense interests that fade with time? Or can you trust that when something grabs your attention, it's likely to hold? I'm not saying that you have to make a lifetime commitment to whatever job you choose next, but one of the objectives of working through your divorce is to get to the point where you put it in your past. If you center your career around divorce, you have to be sure you are drawn to it for healthy reasons. Otherwise you end up with a professional life that thwarts your personal development.

The Scary Part of Town

Every town has a scary part and your new town is no exception— except yours actually has two scary parts. Once you know where they are, you can either contain them so they don't spread or navigate around them altogether.

Danger from without. After your divorce, people—some well-meaning, some not—are going to send you the message that they expect you to aim lower now that you are divorced. This message is not always intentional, but that doesn't make it any less harmful.

Some people may suffer from the misimpression that you are permanently impaired because you're divorced, and as a result certain options are no longer available to you. According to this "logic," just as it wouldn't be reasonable to expect a quadraplegic to get certified to teach CrossFit, it wouldn't be reasonable to expect a divorced woman to get a degree in medicine either. Others may think divorce is a "mistake" for which you must pay. Just as higher interest rates and fewer borrowing options are the price one pays for having a home foreclosed on, living in a dumpy apartment and dating a guy named Dwayne who works at AutoZone is the price you pay for getting a divorce.

The other dangerous message is that your life post-divorce is merely a way station between marriages. People who hold this view don't understand that you are complete on your own. As a result, they are constantly wringing their hands over your "manless" state and angling for you to couple up again. In their view, any man—even Dwayne from AutoZone—is better than no man at all.

Your job isn't to determine why people have these misguided ideas. You simply have to be able to identify who they are and then make sure to keep them far away from you. But when these negative messages come from close friends or even family, it can present a huge risk to your emotional well-being. If you can maintain your relationship with these people without internalizing their negative messages, that's fine. If you need to put some distance between you and them to protect yourself, that's fine, too. Just as staying away from someone who has the flu is a necessity for someone with a weakened immune system, staying away from someone who zaps you with negative messages is mandatory while you are transitioning out of your marriage.

If you do encounter this type of negative messaging, here's the antidote: Appreciate the fact that you will never have more autonomy and control over your own life than you do right now. Don't view your new single life as time you have to spend in the penalty box. See it for the glorious opportunity that it is. Take full advantage of this chance to set up your life exactly the way you want it. Not only will you love the life you create for yourself, but you will dramatically increase the odds of meeting people who share your interests and style.

Danger from within. This danger takes the form of garden-variety fear. But just as there are two different kinds of guilt, there are also two different kinds of fear—the good kind and the bad kind. The good kind of fear keeps you from doing something bad, and the bad kind of fear keeps you from doing something good. When you find yourself in the grip of fear, you have to determine which kind you're dealing with so you can know whether to heed it or push past it.

Let's say you've received an offer to be the activities director on a cruise ship. The job sounds really enticing to you, but it would require you to be away from your young kids for months at a time. You're afraid that being gone for long chunks of time during this sensitive transition period would harm your kids' emotional well-being. The kind of fear that keeps you from hurting those who depend on you is the good kind of fear, and you should listen to that. Or say you've always wanted to open a coffee shop but you're afraid doing so would look self-indulgent and flighty. Instead of doing your research to see whether you might be able to turn your dream into a reality, you instead take some office job you really hate. The kind of fear that keeps you from exploring your options and living the life you want to live is the bad kind of fear.

The bad kind of fear tries to imprison you. You just got yourself out of a bad marriage, for heaven's sake. That took some real guts. You didn't get out of one jail only to move into another. Now is not the time to start bowing down to the bad kind of fear. Whether it's a career change, a new hobby, or a side business, this is the perfect time to try something new. Change is in the air. Your schedule has opened up. And God knows you could use something positive to focus on. If your dream is not harmful to you or your kids, and doesn't jeopardize your ability to take care of your family, then go for it.

If you have something you'd like to try and the only thing that is stopping you is fear of either failure or what other people will think or say, woman-up, grow some ovaries, and face those fears head on. Just as you can reverse-engineer your old hobbies to meet your new budget, chances are you can tailor your dream to fit your new life, too. You owe it to yourself to at least explore your options and try to figure out a way to make it work.

It's Not a Contest

As you put the finishing touches on the different features of your future, it's important for you to remember that this is not a contest—not between your old house and your new house, and not between your current life and your ex's life. And if your ex, or some other voice in your head, tries to goad you into thinking that it is, be smart enough not to fall for it.

If you set out to build something healthy and beautiful, you can't help but end up with a wonderful result. But if you are trying to build something simply to show someone else, you will end up with a place that is gaudy, inauthentic, and dysfunctional. At the end of the day, it's not about your bank balance, your zip code, or how much square footage your house has; what matters is your quality of life and whether your house feels like home. The best way to ensure that your house feels like home is to spend quality time in it and fill it with love. Those features are more valuable and long-lasting than a media room any day of the week.

17.

Quality Control
(Targeting Areas That Need Improvement)

I've spent a lot of time debunking negative messages that surround the end of a marriage. We've talked about the importance of controlling your own personal narrative and being impervious to messages designed to make you feel like a failure as a result of your divorce. I've provided strategies for staying strong, upbeat, and forward-focused.

You *are* awesome, but I would be doing you a disservice if I didn't encourage you to take advantage of the incredible opportunity for self-improvement that is now before you. So, once you are shored up emotionally, you should use a wide angle lens to take an honest look at the entire picture, warts and all. This exercise will then enable you to zero in on the areas where you can have real impact and get lasting results.

If you're not ready to tackle this, no problem. Just curl up with a copy of *Chicken Soup for the Divorced Soul* and call me later. But if you are ready to take your divorce recovery to the next level—where the focus shifts away from your divorce and zooms in on close-up of you and your future—then keep reading.

Respect the 80/20 Rule

A few years ago I learned a very important lesson at a party. And no, it wasn't that you should never drink anything called trashcan punch. What I learned that evening was even more helpful: It was about people's potential to improve.

I was waiting to order a drink of the non-trashcan variety when I happened to strike up a conversation with a business consultant named Sandy. At the time, I was general counsel for a small but growing company, so I was curious about the kinds of problems other companies faced and how Sandy helped solve them. In her experience, she said, one of the biggest problems companies had was not knowing how to get the most out of their employees. She wasn't referring to managers who were either not strict enough on the one hand or too strict on the other. She was talking about managers who didn't understand how to maximize their employees' strengths or motivate them to improve their performance.

Sandy explained that the average employee excels at about 80 percent of what she's responsible for doing and struggles with the remaining 20 percent. Not coincidentally, employees enjoy working on projects that require skills they have mastered and dislike working on projects that require skills they lack. Managers often think that to help employees improve they need to make them better at the 20 percent they struggle with. On the surface, this theory makes sense. After all, there's no need to worry about the other 80 percent.

This gets it exactly wrong, according to Sandy. Trying to force an employee to get better at something she has neither interest nor aptitude in is a recipe for frustration and dissatisfaction, but not results. A wiser approach is to zoom out and make two lists, one of all your organization's needs and another of your employees' skills. Don't limit yourself by the job descriptions that are currently in place or notions of who has always done what. Instead, think only about what needs to get done and all the skills your employees have. Then assign the tasks to those who are best suited to perform them. In the end, everyone should have a job description comprised almost entirely of tasks at which they are skilled. If managers go through this exercise and reassign the work accordingly, the end result should be happier employees and a more efficient company.

Sandy's philosophy got me thinking about whether the 80/20 rule could be applied to other aspects of life, not just at the office.

Do what comes naturally. I have always enjoyed projects that involved writing but struggled with organization. I was hard on myself for not being more organized and felt like a failure for not getting the upper hand on that. Sandy's philosophy made me realize that I could sink a bunch of time into trying to develop my organizational skills (and over the years, I actually had), but I would get only minimal results and maximum frustration in return for my efforts. But if I put the same amount of time into developing my writing skills, the payoff would be huge, both in terms of results and satisfaction.

This doesn't mean that I will never have to straighten up my closet or plow through piles of papers on my desk again. It means I shouldn't feel bad that this type of work doesn't come naturally, just as someone else shouldn't feel bad for disliking writing projects. It also means that depending on my workload, income, and the value of my time, at some point it may make sense for me to hire someone to help me keep organized rather than trying to do it myself.

Sandy's philosophy also made me rethink my tendency to label the things that I don't enjoy or am not good at as "weaknesses." No one thinks of Leonardo DiCaprio as having a weakness because the actor does not sing well. No one thinks that Rafael Nadal, one of the world's top-ranking tennis players, should play less tennis so he can dedicate time to shoring up his baseball skills. But many of us keep a running list of not only what we're good at but what we're bad at, too. And often we place more emphasis on the latter.

Let go of what you're not good at. What does all this mean for you? As you shift gears and move forward, try to restructure your workload so that you replace tasks you don't excel at with projects you do. Of course, no one can avoid every task she dislikes. But when it comes to the ones you're stuck with, give yourself a break. Don't fall into the frustrating trap of feeling as if you need to focus on areas where you have little hope for meaningful growth. Instead, put your time and energy into areas for which you have passion or talent. This is where you have incredible capacity for upside. You will get a better return on your investment in every sense.

If you have a gift for foreign languages but cooking isn't your thing, no worries. Spend your time learning Italian, and let Newman's Own provide the marinara sauce for you. It's not realistic to expect everyone to be good at everything, and it's not reasonable for you to expect that of yourself either. The more you can refashion your daily life to showcase the things at which you excel, the higher your quality of life will be as a result.

Avoid standard issues. *Anything worth doing is worth doing well.* That's how the saying goes. But what does that really mean, anyway? "Well" is hardly an objective standard. Anyone who has ever glanced at Pinterest knows that there are millions of different ways to tackle the very same project. A better message is this: Don't miss the chance to do something you enjoy because you're worried about other people's standards.

I have two friends who love to entertain. Sarah hosts dinner parties that would make Martha Stewart proud. From the menu to the table setting, every detail is breathtaking and lovely. Karen's style is the opposite. She cooks up amazing food and has an open-door policy. Many friends on her free-floating guest list bring dishes, too. The various dishes are laid out on the table and kitchen counters. Folks grab plates and silverware, and eat wherever and whenever they want.

Anyone who has been to dinner at either Karen's or Sarah's house knows firsthand that hospitality comes naturally to each of them. They are both social animals. But there's no denying these two have different styles and throw completely different kinds of parties. Karen wouldn't be interested in throwing a party like Sarah's, and vice versa. If either felt she had to throw a party like the other, she'd likely never entertain again. And speaking as a friend of both, I can tell you my social life would suffer as a result.

My point is, whoever is in charge of a project gets to set the standard. If you want to do something, do it according to your own standards—whether those standards are higher, lower, or otherwise different from anyone else's. That way, you'll be in the best position to enjoy the process and be happy with the outcome.

Toss out your hopeless chest. Raise your hand if you remember hope chests. You know, the trunks that were issued to young girls of yesteryear. Girls were supposed to fill their trunks with "must have" items they would need once they got married—things such as dishes, linens, and antidepressants. (In other words, your everyday basics.) The fact that I have to explain this makes me very happy because it tells me that at least one of the ways in which society historically conditioned young girls to be singularly focused on marriage has fallen by the wayside.

Now, if we could just get the hopeless chest to follow suit. The hopeless chest is downloaded into girls' psyches at an early age. It contains a list of skills that girls are expected to master to be worthy wives and mothers. Those skills include housekeeping, cooking, mistake-free parenting, arts and crafts, scrapbooking, photo library science, greeting card communication, in-law diplomacy, and the ability to look stunning at all times. Women who don't master all of them often end up feeling hopeless. (And that's where the antidepressants come in handy.)

Although I have my own set of talents, I have no real aptitude for many of the skills contained in a typical hopeless chest. For decades I struggled with feeling like a substandard wife and mother. I was spotty at greeting card communication. I chronically underperformed when it came to maintaining the family photo albums. And my scrapbooking capabilities were nonexistent.

I did plenty of other things that weren't on the list. I made up long stories involving my kids' favorite imaginary characters. I took them canvassing for political candidates so they could experience grass-roots democracy firsthand. I brought them to local theater productions and other community events. We spent tons of time together doing many interesting things. It wasn't that I thought these things didn't count at all, but I felt they did nothing to help me meet the minimum standards for being a good wife and mom.

After countless cycles of trying, failing, and beating myself up, I eventually realized I was never going to master these skills. It wasn't a question of time and effort; it was a question of basic ability. I finally saw how absurd it was to put so much emphasis on these specific skills. It's not that there is anything wrong with the skills in the hopeless chest; it's just that there is nothing essential about any of them. A kid could easily have a rich and loving childhood with a mom who possessed an entirely different set of skills than the ones in the hopeless chest.

Like mismatched Tupperware in your kitchen cabinet, your hopeless chest is worse than useless to you. It actually gets in your way. The sooner you haul this chest and all of its contents to the curb, the better off you'll be. In realistic terms, that means identifying the skills you always assumed you should be able to do well simply because you're a woman. That can vary from person to person because hopeless chests can have regional and cultural differences. For example, because I'm Italian American, my hopeless chest contained the expectation that I would learn the art of making an amazing marinara sauce from scratch. Luckily for both my family and my self-esteem, that was one skill I mastered.

Figure out what tasks have always caused you to feel inadequate as a woman, and stop letting these outdated notions and unrealistic expectations diminish the satisfaction you get from all the things you do well. Appreciate the talents you possess, and admire those you lack when you find them in others instead.

Getting rid of your hopeless chest once and for all will benefit not only you but your entire family. You'll break the cycle of passing this garbage down from generation to generation, which will do your kids and future grandkids a huge favor. And greenlighting your family members to celebrate the strengths and skills they have, rather than fretting over the ones they lack, will lead to a higher quality of life and lower therapy bills for everyone.

Too Much Flawsome

So far, in this chapter alone, you've accomplished three very important things. First, you learned the 80/20 rule, which means you're going to put your time and energy into developing your strengths rather than obsessing over your weaknesses. Second, you committed to doing things according to your own standards, rather than trying to match someone else's. Third, you unloaded that useless hopeless chest, freeing yourself and your kids from the dead weight of bogus expectations that you've been lugging around since you were a little girl. The common theme here is resisting the pressure to focus on skills you don't have to the detriment of the skills you do, and refusing to accept the ridiculous notion that the absence of an aptitude amounts to a weakness.

But there is a difference between a lack of proficiency and an outright flaw. Any meaningful attempt at self-improvement involves taking a look at both the good and the bad. Although you shouldn't obsess over the talents that you weren't born with, you shouldn't ignore the negative habits you've developed all on your own.

Everyone knows about the lesson Goldilocks learned when she broke into the Three Bears' house. There is a downside to being either too soft or too hard, and the sweet spot is between the two extremes—where it's firm but not without some give. But Goldilocks's experience revealed some additional information that you might never have heard about. It involves three different attitudes when it comes to dealing with one's personality flaws.

Papa Bears are fundamentally incapable of owning up to any of their flaws. Papa Bears believe that as long as they don't recognize any of their own faults, no one else will notice them, either. What they don't realize is that their refusal to admit to their flaws not only prevents them from working on any of them but actually makes their list of defects longer. And that extra flaw on the list is impossible to overlook.

Mama Bears are on the opposite end of the spectrum. Rather than ignoring their flaws, they fixate on them too much, which ends up taking a toll on their self-esteem. This preoccupation with their flaws not only clouds their ability to see their own strengths but blocks everyone else's view of them, too. In the end, Mama Bears don't have enough of a spine to sneak up on their flaws, let alone attack them head-on.

Baby Bears recognize they are not perfect, but they have a positive self-image overall. Unlike Mama Bears, they know what their strengths are, but, unlike Papa Bears, they don't deny the existence of their flaws. This healthy amount of self-awareness permits them to work on their flaws without becoming consumed by them.

If you are either delusional like a Papa Bear or dispirited like a Mama Bear, you are not yet ready to tackle working on your faults. Spend your time and energy getting your mind and attitude right instead. Then, once your skin is thicker and your self-esteem stronger, you will be in a position to begin working on the flaws themselves without bruising your self-esteem in the process.

When you're ready to proceed, the first thing you'll need to do is to conduct an inventory of your personality defects. After all, you can't remediate your flaws unless you know what you're dealing with. Here are the steps to follow:

1. **Make a list of all your flaws.** It might take you a couple of days to do this. I don't mean two straight days of doing only this— at least for your sake, I hope it doesn't take that long. Choose a day when you have a finite window of time to yourself, but you have something scheduled afterward—preferably something fun. You want to get the list started, but you don't want to dwell on it for too long. Then leave the pen and paper out and add to the list as you think of more things.

2. **Spot-check your list for flaws that are pathological.** If there's anything really egregious—like kleptomania—that will require more help than this chapter can provide. Get a therapist for these issues.

3. **Divide your flaws into two groups: temporary and permanent.** This step isn't rocket science. Permanent flaws are ones that you've been aware of for a long time, and temporary flaws have developed more recently. If for most of your adult life you were a social drinker, but since your divorce you've

taken to throwing back three or four cocktails each night, this flaw goes on the temporary list. But if over the course of your life, you've lost tons of friends due to your tendency to talk about people behind their backs, then gossiping goes on the permanent list.

4. **Rank the flaws on both lists in order of seriousness – baddies at the top, minor infractions at the bottom.** When you are done with your inventory, you should have two lists of flaws that are ranked in order of seriousness (and maybe a new therapist, too).

Confronting Permanent Flaws

When it comes to extra weight you just can't lose, the saying goes, "If you can't lose it, decorate it." The same principle applies here. If you're like most folks, you've tried to address your permanent flaws off and on over the course of your life. And if you're like most folks, you haven't been successful. So, how can you learn to make the most out of living with the flaws you're stuck with? There are three different approaches you can take.

Make quitting your new obsession. If you have an old, pesky habit that is sufficiently serious—such as smoking—you need to focus like a laser beam on quitting, and dedicate whatever resources necessary to getting the support you need to succeed. These habits amount to ticking bombs in your life. You have to deactivate them before they blow you up.

Contain the damage. If your flaw is situational, don't allow yourself to get into the situations that trigger trouble. One of my permanent flaws is that I'm a bad borrower—I lose track of things and then fail to return them. I consider this a pretty serious flaw because it hurts my friendships and my reputation. My strategy for containing the damage is not to borrow things. If a friend offers to lend me a book, I explain my shortcoming and tell her I only take things I'm allowed to keep. You know where your Achilles's heel is, so make sure you don't leave it exposed.

Get good from bad. Some flaws can be mined for potential good. Are you vain? Use your vanity as motivation to get to the gym on a regular basis. Are you egotistical? Buy the recognition you crave by donating money in your name to good causes. The point is, if you are stuck with an unattractive quality, you may as well use it to make life better, not worse.

Tackling Temporary Flaws

When it comes to the baddies at the top of your list of temporary flaws, the sooner you address these, the better. If you wait too long to take on a temporary problem, it will become a permanent one, and permanent flaws are much harder to correct. Smoking cigarettes now and then when you go out with your girlfriends is a temporary habit that you need to permanently kick. You're not just playing with fire. You're playing with fire *and* lung cancer. Surely you can find better things to play with.

When it comes to your minor character defects, keep in mind that no one expects you to be 100 percent flawless. It's up to you to decide which minor flaws you want to take on, and which ones to let slide. Targeting a smaller flaw is an exercise in self-improvement that easily yields positive results and leaves you with an accomplishment you can be proud of. Catholics have a special season for this exercise. It's called Lent. But you don't have to be Catholic to participate. Every year I give up swearing for Lent. But after the Easter Bunny has come and gone, those pesky expletives start hopping right back into my vocabulary. Before I know it, they're multiplying like rabbits again. Rather than getting mad, I take comfort in knowing that I can quit at any time—and it won't be long before Lent rolls around again, anyway.

Minor character flaws are part of being human, so you may as well have some fun with them. Use the ones you're not prepared to shake as a chance to get comfortable with imperfection. When you successfully tackle a flaw, make sure to celebrate your triumph in self-improvement.

18.

Checking Your Rearview Mirror

It's time for a feelings quiz! Are you excited about your future? Are crying jags soooo last season? Have you come to appreciate how much better your life is today than when you were in that Land of the Living Dead that was your marriage? If you answered "yes" to these questions, here is your prize: You get to prepare an accident report on your marriage!

No, I'm not trying to make you have a relapse. And yes, I understand this might strike you as a really lousy payoff for all of your amazing progress. Trust me, there's a method to the madness. This exercise is necessary. And although it won't be fun exactly, it will be rewarding in its own way.

There's a reason why we didn't tackle this no-fun exercise back when you hated life, rather than waiting until you were finally feeling good about things again. You know the warning on your car's side-view mirror about objects being closer than they appear? The same thing goes here. When you are too close to the situation, you lack the necessary perspective to conduct an honest examination of what happened between you and your ex. You need to have temporal and emotional distance to be able to do this right. You have to be past the pain to let go of the tendency to posture and blame.

Your answers on the feelings quiz confirm that you're out of the woods when it comes to your divorce. You have managed to dodge a lot of bullets, and you're healing from the wounds caused by the bullets that you couldn't avoid. But there's a major danger that lies ahead: the danger of getting into another relationship, repeating old mistakes, and having to go through all this all over again. And that would be even worse than a relapse.

Dating has a way of sneaking up on people—even those who vow never to date again. Once you are on solid emotional ground and your divorce is final, you could meet someone at any time. (I bumped into a guy at a restaurant one night when I was having dinner with my extended family. We started dating and over five years later we're still together.) So, it's important to sort through the rubble now rather than trying to do that while you're in the throes of a new relationship. Plus, doing the work at this point will help you to make smarter choices about whom to get involved with the next time. After all, you don't want to end up with the same kind of guy as your ex.

The best defense against repeating past mistakes is to fully appreciate what went wrong in your last relationship, and to totally own your share of the mistakes that were made. Even if your husband was a lying, cheating scumbag and you were nothing but delightful and supportive (and everyone who knew the two of you agrees with this description), you have to examine why you were attracted to someone like him to begin with and/or what warning signs you missed or ignored along the way. But if you're being honest, it's probably not that black and white, and there is plenty of blame to go around. If you truly believe that you didn't do a single thing wrong, you are not ready yet to do this work—and you are definitely not ready to date.

Based on the answers to your feelings quiz, I have faith in you. I think you're up to this challenge. If you agree, start your engine, buckle up, and follow the route outlined below.

Dangerous Conditions

The first step is to inventory the baggage that you and your ex owned before you met each other, because this baggage was likely one of the factors that created the dangerous conditions that led to the divorce. What kind of marriage did your parents have? How about your ex's parents? What was each of your roles within your respective families? What were your past relationships like, including the relationship that immediately preceded this one? When you first met your ex, were you trying to pick someone "opposite" from your last relationship? Or do you always go for a certain type? These are all questions you need to carefully consider.

By way of example, here's what my dangerous conditions report looked like: I was the youngest of five kids and I fully embraced the role of baby. I was generally content to let everyone else be in charge of major decisions. My dad was a volatile first generation Italian American man and my mom had a talent for pushing his buttons. My parents' relationship had two modes:

fighting and not speaking. My brothers and sisters and I spent a lot of time and energy trying not to provoke Dad and hoping Mom wouldn't, either.

Before I met That Man, I was married to someone I thought was the opposite of my dad. My then-husband was not beholden to traditional rules regarding gender roles in relationships. Eventually, I ended up with more education and earning power than he had. He was bohemian and enlightened enough to be totally cool with that, but ultimately I was not. I reacted to that divorce by concluding that the next time around, the traditional marriage model was a must for me.

That Man had a provincial Midwestern upbringing in which his father was the head of the household and his mother played a subordinate role. What his family lacked in volatility, they made up for in a lack of direct communication in the name of civility. Despite the passage of time and progress in the area of gender equality, my ex firmly believed in this old school model of marriage.

When we first starting dating, he was in the beginning stages of divorcing his then-wife, whom he had met in support group a few years earlier. (Consider this entire experience as a cautionary tale for what happens when people date before their divorces are final.) He told me that she was unstable and backed it up with story after story about her crazy behavior. Although things initially seemed to be going well enough between the two of us, he told me that he was "afraid" that I would "turn mean" like her.

The Accident in Slow Motion

Once you've taken a look at the tendencies, habits, and expectations that each of you brought into the relationship, the next step is to take a frame-by-frame look at what happened after you got together. How were things initially? When, why, and how did things start to change? How did each of you handle these changes? What prompted you to get married?

Like a lumber truck driven down a mountain road by a drunk on a rainy day, my ex's and my heavy loads made catastrophe inevitable. I noticed his control issues, intermittent outbursts, and other irrational reactions early on. I assumed this was the toxic fallout of the craziness he had experienced in his brief but thoroughly dysfunctional previous marriage, which he insisted was totally her fault. Rather than setting firm boundaries about how I would allow myself to be treated and what I would put up with, I let a combination of courtesy and cowardice prevent me from drawing too hard a line. My own upbringing (being the baby of a family and having a domineering father) made the situation feel familiar to me. I thought I could avoid any uncomfortable confrontation in the short run, and in the long run he would realize that I was not "mean" or "crazy" like his ex-wife, and then his behavior would normalize. I turned out to be wrong.

Initially, I viewed his approach to marriage as a more modern version of the traditional one, and an improvement over the one I was raised with. But as his efforts to be on his best behavior wore off, I realized what it really was: a more chilling version of my parents' dysfunctional marriage. Perhaps he thought my upbringing, combined with the frustrations of my previous marriage, would make me amenable to a relationship where I had hardly any say. He turned out to be wrong.

After our daughter was born and I stopped working, he ratcheted up both the control and the jerkiness. The more control he seized, the more my resentment grew. But I failed to address it head-on in the interest of keeping the peace. Once that pattern was set, I was unable to change it. For a stretch of years, we lived in the same house but we liked each other less and less.

Eventually, his demands and my disempowerment reached a point at which I could not take it anymore. My sanity and emotional well-being were at stake, and the lessons my kids were learning from our relationship were unacceptable. But my speaking up was not part of our arrangement. When I tried, he took it as a challenge to his "authority."

Determining Liability

Now that you have both inventoried the conditions leading up to the calamity and reviewed the accident frame by frame, you are in a position to assign liability. If you have been honest and thorough in the first two steps, this third step may be obvious, but it will not be easy. You may come away with a long list of things for which your ex is liable, but there will be plenty of things on your list, too. If there isn't, you need to go back to conduct a truth check on the first two steps because you were probably glossing over your shortcomings.

I know that taking a long, hard look at where you went wrong isn't exactly fun. But you know what's even less fun than that? Repeating the same mistakes over and over again. And remember, I'm not asking you to do anything that I didn't do myself. To prove it, here's the assignment of liability for my marriage.

My ex had control and anger-management issues and a raging case of "Who's not honoring me now?" that I can only guess stemmed from deep-rooted insecurity. All of that is on him. These character defects were evident before I married him, yet I married him anyway. I so desperately wanted a storybook traditional marriage that I bought his explanations for his outbursts or, worse yet, made excuses for him. All of that is on me. It was wrong of him to be a controlling jerk, but it was equally wrong for me to allow myself to be controlled by a jerk. For years I accepted his unreasonable rules, and there's no one to blame for that but me.

Also my fault was my desire to somehow reprise my role as baby of the family by letting someone else be in charge of everything. It was as if I wanted a hiatus from the pressure of having everything fall to me. As a well-educated, capable adult, I willingly entered into a relationship in which I was treated like a subordinate at best, and a charge at worst. I have no one to blame for that but myself.

Finally, it was my fault that I didn't push past my discomfort with confrontation and conflict that was forged in childhood. Not only did this discomfort cause me to fail to speak up when I needed to, but also it caused me to send the message that I wasn't open to normal, honest disagreements or arguments because they might be uncomfortable and could even lead to conflict. Without the possibility of garden-variety disagreements, the only communication options left were raging or bottling things up. So, yes, my ex was a jerk. But I was an immature coward who was in denial. In a competition for the most pitiful personality, I'm not sure who would win. Admitting all of this wasn't easy, but it was necessary.

Now that you've gotten a tour of my long list of faults, it's your turn to give me one of yours. Take a deep breath, then gut it up and get on with it.

Defensive Driving

The last step in this process is to make rules for yourself to follow in the future based on what you've learned by reviewing your past. If you've always gone for the guy who's the life of the party and your relationships always leave you feeling as if you have a horrible hangover, then pledge to pick someone who's not likely to be such a headache. If you were the mini-mom in your family who had to take care of your younger siblings and that caused you to end up with a husband who needed you to tell him what to do and when to do it, then make it a point to avoid guys who are looking for a mommy figure.

My rules going forward were these:

1. **I needed to speak up.** That meant I had to have the guts to bring up unpleasant topics, even when it was uncomfortable. It also meant keeping track of when it was my turn and making sure to take it.

2. **I needed to maintain my independence**—and I needed someone who would maintain his, too. That meant I couldn't date someone whose insecurity made him crave a relationship with stereotypical gender roles. At the same time, I didn't want a man who was looking for someone to take care of him. In other words, both of us needed to act like adults.

3. **I had to have a relationship that was modeled on equality,** not one that followed a master/slave paradigm. Although healthy relationships involve a certain amount of going along to get along, that only works when both parties are flexible. It can't be that one always gives and the other always takes.

4. **I needed to learn what to bring up and what to let go.** It was okay to let little things slide, but only if I could really let them go rather than simply stuffing them down. Things that get stuffed down don't disappear; they fester.

5. **I had to have someone who wanted a mutual admiration society,** not someone who needed a fan club. It was okay to be really into someone, but only if he was equally into me, too. It couldn't be that we only did things designed to feed his ego, such as donating money to his alma mater in his name, but never did anything to build me up.

6. **I had to address things as they arose** rather than telling myself I could fix things later. Just as it's better to keep up with the routine maintenance on your car rather than driving it into the ground and then trying to repair everything at once, it's better to put in the effort to keep your relationship balanced from the beginning. Once rules are agreed to and patterns are set, it's really difficult to change them.

7. **I had to accept that some relationships weren't meant to be.** If I found myself dating someone who wasn't okay with these new principles, rather than making it my job to convince him that my way was the right way, I needed to realize he wasn't the right fit for me. Ending a relationship that wasn't working didn't make me a quitter; it made me honest and mature.

When I first started dating after my divorce, I worked hard to implement these rules. I made it a point to keep things equal and figure out what was okay to let go of and what I had to bring up. At first I overcorrected and brought everything up and let nothing go. But eventually, I found the right balance.

Like using a new computer, doing something a different way requires a lot of conscious effort at first. But if you work at it long enough, your brain adjusts to the new routine and it eventually becomes second nature. The same is true with re-programming your approach to relationships. At first, you will have to fight the tendency to slip back into your old habits. If you keep working on it, though, you will eventually internalize the new approach. When you get to that point, you will be so glad that you persevered, because your reward will be a healthy life—whether you're in a relationship or not. The payday is well worth the effort.

PART FIVE:

COUNTDOWN TO LIFTOFF

19.

Safety Rules for the Post-Divorce Dating Pool

(How to Avoid Mr. Wrong)

Contrary to what you may think, post-divorce dating can actually be a wonderful experience. You've been through hell and you've worked hard to learn and grow from it. You've emerged a stronger person with a clear sense of where you went wrong in the past and where you'd like to go in the future. You are building an amazing life and filling it with people and activities that you love. You're not interested in getting into just any old relationship, but you might be open to the right relationship. Because you are strong and healthy on your own, you know you don't have to stress out about this, and you're in a position to be choosy.

In this chapter, I'm going to go over some criteria for you to consider when you are trying to determine whether someone is relationship material. I'm not going to waste your time boring you with one-size-fits-all rules about how many years older or younger than you a man must be in order to be datable. I'm also not going to rehash old theories about what it means if a man is over a certain age and has never been married. And you don't need me to tell you it's a good sign when a man treats his mother well, but a bad sign if they are so close that he needs her to sing him a lullaby on the phone every night before he drifts off to sleep. You can debate those topics with your girlfriends over cocktails and reach your own conclusions.

But there are a few points you should seriously consider:

Make the right list. Being choosy is great, but make sure you're focusing on factors that actually matter, rather than fixating on things that don't. Before I started dating my ex, I carefully crafted a list of what to look for in a boyfriend. On paper, That Man met all my requirements:

- He was the right political party.
- He was within ten years of my age.
- He had been married before.
- He didn't have kids of his own but was open to trying.
- He had a professional job.
- He wore shoes in the grocery store.

He even got some bonus points for being vegetarian and coming from a big Catholic family. But my list didn't contain a single question that would provide any insight into whether he was nice. If you're going to go to the trouble of making a list, make sure you put the right things on it. Which brings me to my next point.

Love *isn't* all you need. I hate to break it to you, but the Beatles were wrong. When it comes to the list of characteristics that a person should consider, there are qualities that are universal— things that should come preprinted on the potential partner checklist, so to speak. Those items include being honest, trust- worthy, responsible, and—my personal favorite—nice. The rest of the qualities have to be custom-tailored to the person who is making the list. In other words, the checklist is a two-part form. Love matters, to be sure. But if you stop there, without putting pencil to paper and completing the entire analysis—both the preprinted and the custom-tailored portions—you haven't even started your homework, let alone finished it.

Not only will the items on each person's individual list vary, but their ranking of importance will, too. You may love to travel and initially have that on your list, but, if you find someone who has 90 percent of the other items on your list yet is afraid of flying, you may decide that travel is something that you can let slide. Then again, if you are a travel writer and your extended family lives overseas, that item might be nonnegotiable.

Beware of the low bar. My ex used to fly into rages at the smallest provocation. Running around after him apologizing to people for his behavior became almost a full-time job. One time—and I'm not making this up—when I went to apologize to a store clerk who had been verbally lacerated by my ex a few days earlier, the clerk beat me to the punch and apologized *to me*. When I told him he was the one who was due an apology, he explained that he felt sorrier for me since I was married to him. I realized he was right, so I accepted his apology.

Your Game Plan for Kickoff

I realize you've dated before, but I also know it's been a while, and that may make you a little nervous. Not a lot has changed out there—and that's both comforting and discomfiting. I know you're going to do fine with this, but there are some stylistic and attitude adjustments I want you to make to maximize the chance that your first couple of dates will be both fun and fruitful.

Don't discount online dating out of hand. The longer you were married, the higher the likelihood that you will have a skeptical view of online dating. It's time for you to update your impression. Online dating is a viable way to meet people. It's fine to decide it's not for you, but make sure you're vetoing it for legitimate reasons and not a baseless aversion.

The most obvious advantage of online dating is this: Rather than leaving it to chance that you might meet someone through a friend or at the supermarket, online dating provides a pool of people who are interested in dating. An additional advantage is you can get to know a lot about a person before you ever have to meet him. And based on what you find out, you can decide whether you want to meet at all. True, people can present a false front, but that's not a risk exclusive to online dating; pretending to be someone you're not is as old as dating itself. You should exercise caution and discretion when meeting anyone new, whether the introduction is virtual or face-to-face.

Be yourself. The onset of any relationship usually involves a fair amount of image crafting by both parties, and that's understandable. It's only natural to want to make a good impression, but be careful not to do this at the expense of being yourself. It's one thing to be open to trying new things, but it's another to pretend you like things you don't. If you want to be the best "you" possible, go right ahead. But if you are trying to be someone you're not, you're not doing anyone any favors.

It's a date, not a sales call. Because we've been raised to think "catching a man" is our top objective, women often approach dating as a prolonged marketing campaign. Under this mind-set, each date becomes a sales call. Success is defined as getting asked out again, and the ultimate goal is sealing the deal by getting asked to walk down the aisle. When you view dating this way, it costs you the chance to take advantage of the real opportunity presented by each date: an occasion to see if you actually enjoy this person's company. By spending your time trying to sell, you forget to consider whether you're even interested in buying in the first place.

It's about your future, not your past. Dating is the last step in your divorce recovery—a step you shouldn't take until you are done working through your divorce and ready to move forward with your life. Nothing says you're not there yet like spending your first couple of dates droning on about your previous relationship. I'm not telling you this because I'm trying to help you make a good impression. I'm telling you this because I want you to have a good time. Start where you are today and move forward, not backward. Initial dates are a chance for both of you to figure out if you enjoy spending time with each other. If you do, you will likely see each other in the future and there will be plenty of opportunities to fill each other in on things that

▶

▶

happened in your past. There's no need to waste your first couple of dates on that.

Look for a partner, not a prince. After a bad marriage and a nasty divorce, some women come away with the idea that they are going to hold out for Prince Charming next time around. The problem with this goal isn't only that it is outdated and unrealistic; it's lopsided and one-dimensional, too. You want someone who will see you for the multifaceted person that you are and value that complexity, not someone who is looking for a superficial Disney princess. And to get all that, you have to recognize and value the same complexity in him. If you want to be valued rather than rescued, you should look for a partner, not a hero.

Keep an open mind. Most of us have preconceived notions of what we're looking for, but try to keep an open mind. It's one thing to be clear and upfront about your personal deal breakers, but it's another to count something as a negative simply because it's different than what you expected. For example, if you are a Sarah Palin groupie, dating a yellow dog Democrat is not likely to be your cup of tea. But if you always assumed you'd date a guy with an office job, but find yourself going out with an artist, that doesn't necessarily have to go in the negative column. There's no point in continuing to see someone who you know is not a match, but, if a date ends up being a mixed bag of things that you like and things you're not sure about, there's no harm in giving it a little more time.

Given this track record, you can imagine my surprise when That Man didn't unleash his wrath on a sandwich artist at Subway when he went all Jackson Pollock with the mustard after my ex had expressly told him he was a mustard minimalist. Later, I reported the good news to my son. Aaron, who had seen plenty of this behavior and had even been on the receiving end of some of it, did not seem impressed.

"Aaron, you know how he usually comes undone over stuff like that. I mean, this time he didn't—he kept it together. That's big," I explained, a little irked that I had to explain the obvious.

"Whatever, Mom. I guess I don't believe in rewarding normal behavior," he told me. "No one should get a prize for *not* coming unglued when his sandwich order gets screwed up. You get jerk points awarded when you don't manage to keep it together; but you don't get points for good behavior when you simply handle things like a normal person."

When Aaron put it like that, it was hard not to agree.

If you are coming out of a marriage in which your ex was routinely a jerk, you might not realize how easy you are to impress. My boyfriend, Clint, is both affable and easygoing. When we first started dating, whenever we'd hit a bump in the road—a flight was delayed or a suitcase was lost—and he rolled with the punches rather than throwing some of his own, I would shower him with compliments about how awesome he was. Clint would always shrug it off and say, "I like the low bar."

He had a point. Years of living with a guy who wasn't nice lowered the bar for whoever came next and that created a windfall for Clint. It transformed his everyday nice guy behavior into something spectacular in my eyes. Luckily, Clint really *is* spectacular. But what if I had ended up with a guy who was less of a jerk than my ex, but a jerk nonetheless? I wonder if I would have thought he was awesome or if I would have recognized that his behavior was unacceptable. The takeaway is to make sure that your standards are not skewed by your previous experience. It's okay to appreciate the difference between what you used to deal with and what you now enjoy. But your standards for what you'll put up with need to be based on what is actually reasonable, not what seems good only in comparison to how your ex used to act.

Don't give love unconditionally. When it comes to your love life, unconditional love is the equivalent of relationship kryptonite. It is the number one killer of healthy, balanced relationships. So, in case you've been hoping to find someone to love unconditionally, and who will love you unconditionally in return, knock it off.

In case this sounds crazy to you, hear me out. I love Clint. I can't imagine not having him in my life. But I love him because of the kind of person he is and how he treats the people in his life—including me. He is a man of incredible integrity and has a huge heart. I fell in love with him because of these qualities. (Plus, he's easy on the eyes.)

If my assessment of Clint turns out to be wrong—either because he changes or I was just plain mistaken—my feelings for him would also change. Let's say I found out that he was a big fat cheater or stole Social Security checks out of senior citizens' mailboxes. Then I would have no choice but to conclude that he was not the man I thought he was. I'd be crushed by the discovery and mourn the loss of the boyfriend I thought I had, but I would not keep dating him.

When you nail an interview and land a job, you don't get to keep it regardless of what you do from that point forward. Your performance matters. It is evaluated from time to time and your future with your employer depends on how well your boss thinks you're doing. If you stopped showering, shirked your duties, left your trash all over the office, or started berating your coworkers, you would likely get canned. Not surprisingly, people generally care about how they come across at work. But a lot of those same people don't apply the same ethic to their personal relationships. Don't believe me? Then how do you explain the existence of fanny packs and cargo pants? No self-respecting man or woman who is even mildly interested in dating would consider wearing either. But plenty of folks who have exchanged vows of unconditional love rock these items without hesitation.

Conditions are a good thing. They set standards and keep things clear. And they shouldn't be in fine print; they should be in all caps, boldface, 20-point font. So, figure out what your conditions are and be upfront about them. Your relationship will be better because of them.

He must play well with others. When you meet someone new, pay attention to what kind of relationships he has and watch for extremes. When it comes to how he gets along with his family, you're not looking for some *Leave It to Beaver* level of fake perfection. If he is estranged from his mom, has a big brother or a younger sister with whom he had a falling out a few years ago, or a dad who was never really in the picture, that's one thing. But if he has all of the above, that's another. Not speaking to (or constantly fighting with) his family is a red flag.

On the other end of the spectrum, if he is so close to his family that he can't do anything without asking everyone's permission (or inviting everyone along), that's a problem, too. What you're looking for is someone who managed to transition from childhood to adulthood while still keeping his family relationships intact.

When it comes to friends, it's generally a good sign if he's open to mixing with your social circle. But if he wants to wholly adopt your group because he doesn't have any friends of his own, that's a bad sign. Unless he has just moved to town, he should have an established social circle of his own.

But you can have too much of a good thing. It's a good sign for him to have friends but a bad sign if he is overly attached to them. You should especially avoid anyone who subscribes to the Seinfeld Model of Friendship. Just like the television show that inspired the name, guys who subscribe to the SMF belong to a group of friends that is unusually close, and all of them generally suffer from arrested development. Healthy adults have close friends, but, when their romantic relationships reach a certain point, the bond with their significant other becomes tighter than the bond with their friends.

Members of an SMF wholly reject this premise, clinging to the "bros before hos" philosophy long after graduating from high school. Loyalty to the group always comes first. A girlfriend of a guy in an SMF will never gain full membership status in the friendship circle, and she can never fully trust her boyfriend, either. But there is one thing she can count on: All of her personal business will be shared with the entire group, down to the smallest, most intimate detail. Unless you're cool with that, steer clear of any guy who is involved in an SMF.

One last thing to watch for: If he has nothing but terrible things to say about not just his last significant other, but every one of his former significant others, that is a major warning sign. I'm not saying he needs to be besties with all his exes—because that, too, is a red flag. But he should be able to break up and move on without demonizing every single one of them.

Be a smart shopper. If you buy a pickup truck, you can't later complain that it's not a sedan. Similarly, if you start dating a man who loves to spend his weekends watching ESPN, you can't complain when he's not interested in going in with you on season tickets to the opera. Rather than trying to change someone into being the person you want him to be, pick someone who has similar interests in the first place.

No sale is final. Dating is like a "try before you buy" period. Use it as an opportunity to get to know each other. If it turns out the two of you aren't all that compatible, there is no shame in recognizing this and deciding to go your separate ways, but there is shame in staying in a relationship that isn't really working. Doing so is as futile as it is frustrating. It's better to cut your losses and move on. Remember, you don't have to be in a relationship all of the time. You've learned how to have a rewarding life on your own. It's easier to enjoy life and find the right match when you're not tangled up in a mismatch.

Evaluating outside data. When it comes to your friends and family's reactions to your new love interest, the weight you give to each opinion should correspond to the amount of good sense the person issuing the opinion has. So, if your shallow friend, whose only criteria for a boyfriend are looks and bank balance, thinks your new NPR reporter boyfriend is unacceptable because he's boring and shabby, you should either give her opinion no weight at all, or even count it as validation of your choice. But if your smart, sensible sister thinks that your new boyfriend talks to you in a condescending tone, you should think about that.

Keep in mind, however, that if you have a track record of picking losers, your friends and family may be predisposed to distrust your next choice, even if he's smart, kind, funny, and handsome. If you have confidence in your choice, proceed with caution while giving everyone the time and opportunity to get to know him. Time will prove which one of you is right—and as long as you've done your homework, my money is on you.

20.

Don't Get Fooled Again

(Advice for Dating After You've Been Cheated On)

Navigating a new relationship after getting cheated on can be a tricky business. You might have a couple of nagging questions holding you back: Has the betrayal you experienced in your last relationship affected your ability to trust someone in the future? And perhaps more important, should it? Those are excellent questions. Although it's wise to learn how to avoid making the same mistakes in the future, you don't want to give them so much weight that they keep you shackled to your past.

President George W. Bush once said, "Fool me once, shame on—shame on you. Fool me—you can't get fooled again." (Or as the sentiment is often less eloquently put, "Fool me once, shame on you. Fool me twice, shame on me.") So true. The fact that you got cheated on was not your fault. But it will be your fault if you repeat the same mistakes the next time around.

The following tips can help you avoid that trap.

Forgive but don't forget. Wait! Let me explain. I'm not talking about forgiving *him*; I'm talking about forgiving *yourself* for your own lapses in judgment. Maybe you believed him when he said the only reason he went to the topless bar every day was because the strip steak special just couldn't be beat. Or perhaps you ignored the story you heard from a mutual friend about how his last relationship ended when his then-girlfriend found a half-empty box of condoms tucked in the suitcase he took on his frequent business trips. Maybe you thought you could change him. Or you didn't listen to your gut when it kept telling you that something was wrong. There are real lessons to learn from all these mistakes. But once you learn them, your job is to forgive yourself while not forgetting what you've learned.

It's not you; it's him. Whatever your shortcomings were, he was the one who cheated, not you. You may have ignored the warning signs, but that goes in the category of letting yourself down; it doesn't rise to the level of betraying someone else's trust. In terms of culpability, there's a big difference between those two offenses.

Don't let his betrayal change the essence of who you are. If you're a trusting person by nature, that's a good thing. But if you're a trusting person who ignores red flags, change the part about ignoring red flags. In other words, *do* let the experience generate healthy growth, but *don't* let it rob you of your positive qualities.

Get a new type. If you're a person who has a "type" and your ex is a representative sample, it may be time to get a new type. If you have a history of being attracted to guys who are players, you won't be entitled to any sympathy points if you date another guy with a "bad boy" reputation and he ends up cheating on you, too. So, before you dive back into dating, think about what you want from your love life. Do your spirits soar at the thought of turbulence or do you like smooth sailing? Once you have the answer to this question, pick a guy who's interested in traveling in the same manner and direction, but understand that, if you buy a ticket for a bumpy ride, you can't be surprised when you get a crash landing.

Don't convict the wrong guy. Once you start dating someone new, don't expect him to serve the sentence for the crimes committed by your ex. There is no faster way for you to kill your next relationship than to send your new boyfriend the message that you expect him to cheat on you any second—or, worse yet, to treat him as if he already has. Neither the victim vibe nor a passion for payback is attractive to healthy individuals. If Beaten-Down Becca is your post-breakup persona, you should automatically be suspect of any new suitors because healthy guys don't go for the victim type. And if you are a Vengeful Vanna, dedicated to punishing your new boyfriend for the pain caused by your last one, you can expect another round on the relationship Wheel of Misfortune.

The bottom line is this: If you are not at the point at which you can let a new relationship grow without poisoning it with your past experience, then save everyone the trouble and don't date yet, because you are not ready.

Check your suitcase for emotional baggage. After you break up with a cheater, there are two nasty parting gifts that often sneak into your suitcase when you pack your stuff. One is fear and the other is insecurity. Fear that someone might cheat on you again can make you skittish of emotional vulnerability—a necessary component in any healthy relationship. That fear can cause you to cut and run rather than move forward with a relationship that has real potential. And insecurity about your own self-worth and the prospect of being alone can keep you from breaking it off with someone you know is not good for you. You've heard of gifts that keep giving. Well, these are gifts that keep taking. Sort through all your stuff to make sure that these two saboteurs aren't stowed away, waiting for the chance to undermine your prospects for healthy relationships in the future.

Conventional wisdom holds that cheaters never win. For the purposes of this chapter, I would offer this slight variation: "Cheaters never win—unless you let them by failing to learn and move on." Do your part. Don't let the cheaters win.

21.

Rules of Engagement
(How to Balance Post-Divorce Dating and Your Kids)

This is a good news/bad news situation. The good news is now that your divorce is final and the temporary insanity that it caused has passed, you're ready to consider another relationship. The bad news is that next to divorce, getting into a new relationship is the second leading cause of temporary insanity.

I'm not trying to be a buzzkill here. A new relationship can be an exhilarating and blissful experience. But to avoid putting yourself and your kids through another round of family drama, you have to be very aware of what you're doing—just as you were during your divorce.

Here are some guidelines to help you steer clear of trouble.

Don't fast forward. That initial phase of a new relationship can be one of the most amazing rushes ever. Everything about it makes you want to go full speed ahead, taking your relationship from new boyfriend to permanent partner in a matter of days. But because you are a responsible grownup, you know that would be a really stupid thing to do.

After all, you've worked hard to get to where you are today. You remember the living hell that your divorce was. If you really work at it, you can even vaguely remember how you were once head-over-heels in love with your ex. So, you know full well that sometimes things that seem really amazing in the very beginning turn out to be pretty terrible in the end. The last thing you want to do is to jeopardize the life that you have carefully reconstructed for yourself and your kids. So, just as you enjoy a piece of cake one delicious forkful at a time rather than swallowing it whole, take the time to savor each minute of this phase of your relationship rather than rushing ahead.

Don't shortcut character development. Here's a common misstep divorced women make when it comes to new relationships: As soon as they've been on two dates with a guy, they want to introduce him to their children. Your kids have had enough rough sailing. The last thing they need is a bunch of new waves created by moving too fast with your new boyfriend.

Your love life can have a big emotional impact on your kids. If they like the guy, they will form an attachment to him. If you end up breaking up sooner rather than later, this sets them up for a loss that was totally avoidable. If they don't like him, your boyfriend can become a wedge between you and your kids, and that creates tension for everyone.

Protect your children and your home life by holding off on the introduction until you're sure it's worth the potential upheaval. Make sure you know him really well and you're reasonably certain he's going to be around for the foreseeable future. I'm talking about a vetting period measured in months, not days. Feel free to date, but try to schedule your dates on evenings when your kids are with their dad or otherwise away.

Don't treat the kids like Oscars. If your new boyfriend has kids, resist the urge to wage a campaign to win them over right away. You may think that getting in good with his children will help impress your new love interest and advance your budding relationship. Not only is this strategy unfair, but it often backfires.

This involves manipulating the emotions of children simply to further your love life. That's a pretty rotten thing to do. It backfires because when you start off acting like a fan rather than a friend, you often end up pretending to be someone you're not. It won't take long for the kids to figure out that you really aren't who you pretended to be, and they will realize you were using them to get in good with their dad. At that point you will have your first obstacle to overcome—and it will be completely your fault.

A better approach is to have the patience to get to know each other gradually. Rather than pretending to like every single thing about his kids, slowly discover what you honestly have in common. You won't like everything about them and they won't like everything about you. But you will all be able to trust that your opinions are honest and the developing relationship is genuine.

Of course, women aren't the only ones who do this. Make sure your new boyfriend doesn't approach your kids as if they are awards that can be won if his performance is impressive enough. Children deserve to be treated like people who are worthy of respect, not prizes that are up for grabs.

Don't hold auditions for replacement parent. Don't encourage your kids to call your new love interest "Dad" or invite his kids to call you "Mom." These kids already have parents, and being told to call someone else Mom or Dad only serves to confuse them or make them feel awkward. It could even cause tension with their actual mom or dad. Instead, model for them what it looks like to approach a relationship in a mature manner— slowly, with respect and restraint. That's a lesson that will serve them well in many ways.

You are the casting director of your love life. Your kids don't get to decide who gets cast as your boyfriend; that's your decision. They *do* get to decide whether they like him, and don't be surprised if they don't at first. Many kids are not thrilled to have a new leading man waltzing into their house and changing the family dynamic. Even though you can't order them to like your new boyfriend, you *can* insist that they treat him with respect while everyone works through the transition. The best way to maximize the chances that your kids will eventually like your boyfriend is to be selective about whom you choose, carefully vet him before you make any introductions, and then continue to take things slowly once you do.

Handling negative reviews. If your kids don't like your boyfriend, give them a chance to explain the basis for their opinion. If they tell you that he gives them a creepy feeling, they caught him rifling through your jewelry box, or he told them his dream is to have a snake farm and your backyard would be a perfect location for that, these are serious complaints that you should heed. But if they say he is an attention hog or that you really don't need a boyfriend because you have them, that's a different story. Complaints of this nature indicate that their objections aren't based on anything specific to him, but rather they dislike the idea of your having any boyfriend at all.

It's easy to understand why. After all, these are your kids. From their standpoint, there's a pretty big gross-out factor when it comes to the idea of their mom being all starry-eyed over some guy and doing all those things that go along with dating. And what kid wouldn't get her back up over some new guy cutting in on the time and attention she gets from her mom?

Their complaints might be understandable, but that doesn't make them legitimate. There's no need to stop seeing someone over unfounded complaints. In fact, doing so would send your kids the message that they have ultimate authority over your love life, and that would set a precedent you would quickly come to regret. Although breaking it off isn't wise, making some adjustments to take the pressure off everyone would be a very smart move. Continue to see your boyfriend, but go back to seeing him away from the house and/or at times when your kids are not around. Don't hide the fact that you're continuing to see him; just don't include your kids in your plans.

Over time, your kids will adjust to the idea of your having a boyfriend and their resistance will most likely diminish. Then you can slowly ramp up the occasions when your boyfriend is included in family events. A side benefit of this approach is it affords you additional time to get to know him, which means you will be that much more sure of things before he gets involved in your kids' lives. Your reward for being sensitive to their needs is that your kids will be far more likely to actually like your new flame (rather than merely tolerating him) if they don't feel he is being forced on them. And all that gives your relationship a greater chance of succeeding.

Don't give your kids a supporting role. Every relationship—even a brand-new one involving a guy you are totally smitten with—has its share of bumps in the road. Because you're coming off a divorce and you haven't dealt with the dynamics of a new relationship in a very long time, it's natural for you to want to process these developments by talking them out with someone to get a little perspective. That's fine, as long as that someone is not one of your children. Just as you leaned on your A-Team during your divorce, you need to turn to your friends when you want to dish about your new love life.

You may feel that talking to your kids about your dating life makes you look cool or bonds you together in a new way, but it really constitutes inappropriate sharing. It could cause your kids to see you more as a teenager and less as a parent, and that will diminish their respect for you and your authority with them. Consider also that they will be predisposed to take your side in any spats you have with your boyfriend, and that can interfere with their relationship with him in the long run. You and your boyfriend may kiss and make up, but your kids may find it hard to forgive and forget.

Have a heart-to-heart with your new heartthrob. Before you and your boyfriend meet each other's kids, you should talk about these points to make sure you are both on the same page. If you do not feel comfortable enough with him to have that conversation, you do not know him well enough to introduce him to your kids. If you find yourself more worried about how he will react than how your kids are going to be treated, that's a pretty clear sign that you're suffering from temporary insanity. When you put concerns about your new relationship ahead of concerns for your children, you need to spend less time dating and more time thinking about your priorities.

When it's time for your next creative collaboration, these guidelines should ensure that you end up with a romantic comedy rather than a horror movie. And after that divorce film noir of yours, something upbeat and family-friendly is exactly what your audience is craving.

22.

Healthy Ever After

You. Have. Arrived! You have completed one of the biggest challenges that life will ever throw your way. And not only have you survived, but you have thrived. You've learned, you've grown, you've made mistakes—and you've learned and grown from those mistakes, too.

No, I'm not forgetting about the last leg of your personal triathlon. I realize you have only completed two events—you swam across the river of sewage, and then you cycled away from its putrid banks toward the outskirts of your beautiful new future, which is where you now stand.

This final stretch involves living the rest of your life to the fullest, so it's technically not part of your divorce. This event will be completed on foot and your pace will vary depending on the course. Sometimes you will full-on sprint; other times you will jog. There will be stretches where you hike uphill and others where you amble downhill. You will encounter junctures where you'll need to decide which road to take, or you might even decide to make your own road. At times, you'll want to stop and enjoy the view or rest for a spell. But I hope you don't waste too much time just sitting around or, worse yet, looking back over your shoulder.

If you're feeling anxious about this final leg, that's normal. But don't worry. You are well equipped to handle the road ahead. You are fully capable of artfully maneuvering around the curves, straightaways, inclines, and declines. You have finished something perilous and demanding, and you're still standing tall. That means you are now a full-fledged Emotional Hardbody— someone with the smarts, strength, and know-how to roll with life's punches. You can enjoy the good times and weather the difficult ones without falling apart. You should not only own your Emotional Hardbody status, but you should totally rock it.

To get the most out of being an Emotional Hardbody, you need to familiarize yourself with the following owner's manual.

Your mood settings. Just because your divorce is over, do not expect to be happy all the time. As an Emotional Hardbody, you have a full range of possible moods—from elated and ecstatic at the top end to furious and despondent at the bottom. Your mood will shift around depending on what is going on in your life, and that is completely normal.

Negative readings. When your dial goes negative, don't panic. Know that the mere fact that you are experiencing a negative emotion isn't in and of itself an indication that something is wrong. In fact, it is a sign that you are normal. If you are sad or mad and you know the cause (say, you're sad because your cat died or you're mad because your best friend flaked out on you at the last minute and you had to go solo to that "cooking for two" class you signed up for as a team), ride out the feeling. It's perfectly okay to have a negative reaction when something bad happens. Take comfort in the fact that this experience will help you to appreciate happy times all the more.

Refueling your system. When you go through hard times, realize that the scraps and remnants of these tough experiences serve as emotional compost for you down the road, nourishing your relationships, strengthening your roots, and stimulating new growth. Just as your divorce ultimately made you better and stronger, subsequent challenges will, too. Although this knowledge won't make future ordeals any less difficult to get through, there is comfort in it nonetheless.

The Happy Trap. Your goal is to be healthy, not happy. The expectation that you should always be happy puts constant pressure on you. Whenever you experience any emotion other than happiness, you feel as if something is wrong. Staying in this mode of expectation causes unnecessary wear and tear on your system. If you find that you expect to feel happy all the time, that means you have gotten caught in the Happy Trap and you need to reboot your system so you can reset your expectations.

Adding an attachment. There's nothing like a new relationship to turn your happiness setting all the way up to eleven. This is both normal and really fun so you should enjoy every second of it. But just because your relationship starts out on this setting doesn't mean that this will (or should) be its baseline. A realistic baseline for a healthy relationship hovers around content and satisfied (which is not at all the same thing as settling, by the way). From that baseline, you can expect your mood to go up as well as down—and all of that is completely normal.

Most important, understand your significant other's job is not to be your personal butler of bliss any more than it is your job to be his. In addition to the times that you are blissfully happy, make sure to recognize the times that you are satisfied with each other or content with the relationship, and enjoy these as well. Savoring all these moments will help you to weather the times when you are crosswise at each other or in a rut. And those negative emotions will, in turn, help you to more fully appreciate the positive ones. It's all part of having a full-spectrum relationship.

If you bail on your relationship when you hit a rough patch or try to avoid feeling any emotion other than full-throttle happiness, you are cheating yourself out of a life with real depth and dimension. You are sentencing yourself to an emotional diet that is the equivalent of only eating "food" out of a vending machine. It may taste good for a little while, but it's unhealthy and eventually it will make you sick.

The next generation. When it comes to your own kids, rather than striving to make them happy, help them to develop the tools they need to be emotionally healthy instead. Raise them with the expectation that being normal and well-balanced means experiencing a wide range of feelings. That range includes happiness to be sure, but it includes a lot of other feelings, too.

Your lifetime warranty. Every Emotional Hardbody has a lifetime warranty. Provided that you properly maintain your system by refueling regularly and calibrating your expectations, you should stay balanced and strong for the rest of your life. If you hit a glitch, refer to this owner's manual to debug your system. It's taken a considerable investment on your part to acquire your Emotional Hardbody. The time has come for you to fully enjoy all of the rewards.

Epilogue

● ● ●

The Shelf Life of an Intense Friendship

In the last scene of the movie *Speed*, after everyone is out of danger and the bus finally blows up, the force of the explosion leaves Jack (played by Keanu Reeves) and Annie (played by Sandra Bullock) lying on the pavement, one on top of the other. At long last, they end up kissing. Then Jack says to Annie, "I have to warn you. I've heard relationships based on intense experiences never work."

Jack has a point. Intense experiences often generate relationships that are incredibly close but surprisingly brief. When I was pregnant, I formed really tight friendships with both the instructor and the other moms in the childbirth class I attended. We saw each other in class, and we often got together outside class, too. But over time, every single one of those friendships fell by the wayside. Ditto for the friends I made during the eighteen months or so I spent taking my baby daughter to Gymboree. Those moms and I formed playgroups and hosted each other in our homes at least once a week. Now we've all gone our separate ways.

There wasn't any sort of falling out. It's just that despite our varied backgrounds, we were drawn together by the intense challenge that we all faced. We desperately needed each other's company and support to get through the transition. Once we got to the other side, our lives carried us off in different directions. Now, we exchange Christmas cards or occasionally see each other on Facebook, but that's the extent of it.

So it is with you and me. Much like being roommates in a hospital delivery room, we have shared many intense, embarrassing, and personal moments, and those experiences have drawn us closer. When we started, you were lying facedown on the pavement at the beginning of your divorce, and now you are standing tall, poised to embark on the journey that is the rest of your life. (Ugh. I promised both myself and my publisher that I would write the first-ever divorce recovery book for women that didn't include the word "journey" one single time. And I came so close to making it!)

You may not realize this yet, but, as close as we've been, you've reached the point where you don't need me anymore. You have everything you need to make your way forward on your own. But until you recognize that for yourself, I'm here for you. You can keep this book on your nightstand or even carry it around in your purse for as long as you want. There will come a time very soon, though, when you are ready to unload both the book and me. And that will be a day to celebrate.

That's when you'll know it's time to put the book away—either on the top corner of a bookshelf or even in a box in your closet. (But remember where you've put it, because you might want to pull it out from time to time to glance at the passages that you highlighted or the pages that you dog-eared. Like looking at the hairstyles in your high school yearbook, it will remind you of how much things have changed—and for the better.) Once you've put the book away, get out your calendar one last time, grab a pen, and put a huge heart on that day to symbolize that you are operating at 100 percent again.

You got this book to break free from the divortex, and you have. Your training is officially complete. You are strong, smart, and healthy, and that's one sexy combination. Your new life has begun. You are finished with this book, but a new story—*your* story—has just begun.

Acknowledgments

I wanted a catchy slogan for the acknowledgments for this book—a saying that sums up my sentiments for having gotten this project to the finish line. The Republicans had one during the 2012 presidential election. It was a retort to President Obama's assertion that no success is truly self-made because there are always others who helped along the way. Republicans stood their ground when it came to getting sole credit for their accomplishments and the slogan "I built this" was born.

My feelings are exactly the opposite. This book was much more of an ensemble production than a solo act. But because the saying "It takes a village" is already taken by Hillary Clinton, I guess I'll just go with "There's no 'I' in 'team.'"

This book was a team effort if ever there was one. It began, of course, with my own terrible divorce. I'm not sure how I would have made it through those first few months without the rock-solid support of my sisters and brothers—Angela (or my mini-mom, as I like to call her), Monica, Peter, and Michael. I am so grateful to have these folks—and their significant others and kids—in my life. And there's no telling how long it would have taken me to get back on my feet without the no-nonsense advice I got from my mom and stepdad, Donna and Don. But the limitless love both from and for my two amazing kids, Aaron and Hannah, was what gave me the strength to keep putting one foot in front of the other day after lousy day until things finally got better.

In addition to my own nightmare divorce, inspiration for this book also came from friends and clients who have shared their divorce experiences with me over the years. These women amaze me every day with their honesty, strength, resilience, and humor. Some of the experiences they have shared served as creative inspiration for the fictionalized composites in this book.

Then there are those who helped to convert the inspiration for this book into a reality. A heartfelt thanks to all the amazing folks at Sandra Dijkstra Literary Agency, but most especially to Jill Marr, who has listened to my ideas and provided feedback on how to shape them ever since I cornered her at that conference back in 2010.

Thanks, also, to my publisher Seal Press and especially Laura Mazer, who agreed that women who are not content to simply hug their inner unicorns deserve a book that offers a fresh approach to divorce recovery. Without Laura's agreement, you would not be reading this book right now. (And if it turns out you don't like it, feel free to blame her as well.) And special props to my editor Stephanie Abarbanel for her organizational wizardry, polishing magic, and abundance of patience in putting up with me. Then there's my copy editor, Beth Partin, whose light touch and easygoing style make me want to be more like her someday.

And, Tabitha Lahr, my graphic designer, will always have a special place in my heart. Just like a pair of Lululemon leggings—and I'm talking about the good kind, not the ones that should have flunked the quality control test—they make everything look soooo much better!

At the risk of sounding snarky, I would also like to give a special shout-out to my ex-husband for his intractability—and I mean that (almost completely) sincerely. If he had been willing to make only the smallest of compromises, I would likely still be married to him today, and I would have never learned the extent of my own strength or the degree to which I could be happy.

And, of course, a huge, heartfelt thank-you to my awesome boyfriend, Clint Harbour. His intelligence, selflessness, sense of humor, and huge dimples add immeasurable joy to even the most average of days.

And finally, many thanks to divorcing women everywhere for their willingness to learn what they can from the past, muster their strength, and embrace the future. There may not be an I in "team," but I have located both an M and an E in there. And I'm really thrilled about that, because nothing makes me happier than being a part of this unbeatable team.

About the Author

© Michael Sterling

Christina Pesoli is a writer, breakup coach, and relationship expert. She is the founder of Emotional Hardbody, where she provides training to help women avoid common mistakes that make divorce take longer and cost more. She is a regular blogger for the *Huffington Post*, and her essays have appeared in a variety of publications. She is a proud native Austinite and an even prouder mother of two.

Selected Titles From Seal Press

Ask Me About My Divorce: Women Open Up About Moving On, edited by Candace Walsh. $15.95, 978-1-58005-276-4. A spicy, bracing, riveting anthology that proclaims: I got divorced, and it rocked my world!

Single Mom Seeking, by Rachel Sarah. $14.95, 978-1-58005-166-8. A single mom shares her heartfelt and hilarious take on the challenges of balancing motherhood with singlehood in her search for a good man.

Essential Car Care for Women, by Jamie Little and Danielle McCormick. $17.00, 978-1-58005-436-2. Straightforward, easy to follow, and full of step-by-step diagrams and helpful pictures, this is the ultimate handbook to everything a woman should know about her set of wheels.

The Secret Sex Life of a Single Mom, by Delaine Moore. $17.00, 978-1-58005-386-0. The risqué story of a stay-at-home mom's boundary-pushing experimentations with sex—and resulting self-awakening—after a painful divorce.

Marrying George Clooney: Confessions from a Midlife Crisis, by Amy Ferris. $16.95, 978-1-58005-297-9. In this candid look at menopause, Amy Ferris chronicles every one of her funny, sad, hysterical, down and dirty, and raw to the bones insomnia-fueled stories.

Yogalosophy: 28 Days to the Ultimate Mind-Body Makeover, by Mandy Ingber. $18.00, 978-1-58005-445-4. Celebrity yoga instructor Mandy Ingber offers a realistic, flexible, daily plan that will help readers transform their minds, their bodies, and their lives.

Find Seal Press Online
www.SealPress.com
www.Facebook.com/SealPress
Twitter: @SealPress